THE NEW CROCHET

MARION MADEL

THE NEW CROCHET*

*a beginner's guide, with 38 modern projects

PHOTOGRAPHY BY HIROKO MORI

STYLING BY MAKI NAKAHARA

POTTER CRAFT

NEW YORK

Welcome to the new generation of crochet. From afar, crochet may seem very complicated, but it's actually easier than you think. I recommend you first quickly scan the whole book to get the lay of the land, as though you were a tourist in a foreign country. Read the suggestions, browse the directions, and look at the step-by-step photos. Get familiar with the vocabulary, the symbols, and the basic movements to make crocheted stitches. Then you will dive into the heart of the book, beginning with the first of the 25 lessons, which will help you gradually build your repertoire of crochet skills. Get comfortable in your favorite chair, take your crochet hook in one hand and a ball of yarn in the other. Start by creating a foundation chain, then the slip stitch, and all of the basic stitches in the order in which they are presented. Use the detailed step-by-step photos that illustrate each stitch for more guidance as you perfect your technique. Surprise! You notice that crochet is not all that complicated after all. Now that you are starting to feel comfortable in this new world, you are going to learn another language, one with a specific vocabulary, abbreviations, and a visual way of writing made of circles and lines. After some time, and with practice, you will understand all these symbols at a glance. Are you starting to feel at home here? Take your time and experiment with different kinds of yarn and stitches. Make practice swatches before you begin one of the projects that demonstrates each lesson. These projects are designed to help reinforce the technique you have just learned. The result is a collection of simple, timeless garments and accessories that I hope you'll wear with pride, including oversized scarves, bags, crocheted trims, fingerless mitts, a capelet, and more. Above all, I hope that you will have fun as you unravel the mysteries of this craft and discover how chic and modern crochet can be.

Marion Madel

CONTENTS

BASIC TECHNIQUES

As with any new skill, if you want to take up crochet, you must first learn the fundamentals. Trust me: If you go at your own pace, step by step, and refer to the advice that we give you in this book, you will have all the tools you need. And you'll see that what seems complicated and tedious to you at first turns out, in fact, to be fun and easy. Yes, really! There are certain rules you must follow, but after you learn the basics, the possibilities are limited only by your own imagination.

In this section, we'll review the essential rules, including how to choose an appropriate hook size for your yarn and desired effect, whether you are working in a basic stitch pattern, three-dimensional textures, or exquisite lace. We'll also explore a bit of the vocabulary (chain stitch, double crochet, puff, picot. . .) and the specific symbols used to produce these patterns. As you move forward in this book, you'll have plenty of opportunities to review these methods, and eventually they will be second nature. Every time you crochet a new piece, your skills will continue to evolve. Little by little, you will learn how to polish your technique, tackle more challenging stitches, and nurture your creativity.

SOME NOTES ON YARN AND FIBER

All types of yarn can be crocheted. The choice of a specific type of yarn depends on the project and on the stitch that you are considering using. Are you making an article of clothing or a decorative piece? And if it is an article of clothing, who will be wearing it? Would you use the same yarn for an adult cardigan as for a baby sweater? Depending on the project, you will need a specific type of yarn.

Yarns are widely available in local yarn shops, as well as online (Resources, page 223). They come a vast range of colors updated by the manufacturers seasonally based on current trends.

There are 4 groups of fibers from which yarn is made:
- fibers derived from the plant world,
- fibers derived from the animal world,
- artificial fibers,
- synthetic fibers derived from petrochemicals

Each category of fiber has its own special qualities and characteristics. Yarn may be made of one type of fiber or blended with fibers from the other families.

1 – PLANT FIBERS

Cotton yarn is commonly used in crochet, and is perfect for making lace. Worked very finely, it was traditionally used for embellishing undergarments and baby sweaters.

Slightly heavier weight cotton is used to make doilies and tablecloths in the tradition of Irish filet lace. Cotton possesses undeniable qualities: fine strands, plied tightly that offer great strength. Dyed at high temperatures, cotton has colors that do not bleed. You will find cotton yarns under different names, based on the particular treatments that the fiber has undergone to create yarn with a specialized look and feel.

• **Egyptian cotton** has a smooth, glossy appearance and is made from the longest fibers from the cotton harvest. It is an excellent choice for making crocheted items for your home.

• **Mercerized cotton,** having a lustrous appearance, has undergone a chemical caustic soda treatment that eliminates the imperfections in the fibers and leaves it smoother. It is a fine cotton used for lacework.

• **Perle cotton** often has undergone the mercerization process, which gives it its shiny appearance. Very supple, it is appropriate for making both home decor and summer clothes.

• **Matte cotton** has a less shiny appearance and a very supple and fluffy feel. Yarns made from this kind of cotton are usually made with fewer plies than the other cottons listed above and often are thicker in diameter. It is ideal for making practical clothing like cardigans and pullovers as well as bags.

Linen was used for the finest crocheted European lace until it was replaced with cheaper cotton in the 19th century. Recently, linen has experienced a resurgence of interest thanks to its attractive appearance and durability. Linen has many of the same uses as matte cotton; however, because its fibers are longer and stronger, it is more hard-wearing than cotton.

2 – ANIMAL FIBERS

Wool is a widely used fiber for crochet today. It is used for making both clothing and home accessories. Different kinds of wool feature a diverse range of qualities, as categorized by the Woolmark brand. For example, lambswool comes from a lamb's first shearing when the animal is 6 to 7 months old. "Kid" or "baby" is the equivalent categorization for other animals, such as angora goats or alpacas. It is extremely soft and flexible and is offered either on its own or mixed with other fibers like cashmere or silk. Wool is ideal for cold-weather clothes.

You can also find high-quality **lambswool** and **merino wool,** raised on sheep farms. This wool is composed of sturdy, soft fibers. It works up beautifully in crochet and is usually reserved for making clothing.

One of the most sophisticated and most sought-after animal fibers is **cashmere.** This wool is harvested by combing the downy undercoat of goats from the foothills of the Himalayas. Its rarity is due to the fact that only 100 to 150 grams of fiber are harvested per animal each year. Cashmere is light, soft, and slightly elastic.

On its own or blended, this luxurious fiber works well for crochet and has a lovely drape. Because it is so rare—and therefore more expensive than other materials commonly used in yarn manufacture—cashmere is often produced in skeins of yarn of 25 or 30 grams.

Tweed, meanwhile, possesses the qualities of its original environment, the lands of Scotland and Ireland: tweed yarns are rustic, indestructible, and impermeable, because, in the spinning process, there is a bit of the grease from the fleece of the sheep that ends up on the surface of the strand. It is traditionally used for the famous knitted sweaters from the Aran Isles, but one can also crochet with it very well. Most often available in a bulky or "Aran" weight, it is perfect for making cozy throws and cushions, which are quickly crocheted with big hooks.

There are also feathery fibers often described as "hairy." In this category you'll find **mohair,** which is produced by a goat originating from Turkey, and **angora,** which is a breed of rabbit. It's best to create very simple stitches when crocheting with mohair or angora, because the long, fluffy strands will obscure fancier stitches.

The last type of animal fiber used in yarn is produced by an insect: **silk.** The bombyx silkworm digests the leaves of the mulberry tree and secretes a single, long fiber measuring 765 to 1,300 yards (700 to 1,200 meters) in order to create its cocoon. Silk's softness, flexibility, and sturdiness make a fiber that is suitable for crocheting refined clothing.

3 – ARTIFICIAL FIBERS

Rayon, produced using a process developed by the chemical industry at the end of the 19th century, transforms the cellulose of plant fibers into yarn. Rayon first became very popular in the 1930s with the trend towards artificial materials. Also known as "artificial silk," rayon can be composed of bamboo, soy, ramie, tree bark, and more. Its appearance is very soft, even fluid, and its feel is practically identical to that of silk. When crocheted, it offers an ideal drape for clothing.

4 – SYNTHETIC FIBERS

Thanks to scientific progress, you can crochet with yarns containing metallic fibers, or Lurex. Synthetic microfibers also reduce the yarn's weight when blended with natural fibers like wool or cotton. Polyesters, polyamides, and acrylics are easy to care for and machine washable (a quality lacking in some natural fibers like wool and silk), and have practical thermal qualities. However, some synthetic "novelty" yarns that are too hairy or too fluffy can be difficult to work with. I recommend crocheting a test swatch before jumping into a project with this type of yarn.

CARE INSTRUCTIONS

Although not always the case, guidelines often appear on the ball band. They are indicated by international symbols identical to those used on care labels for textiles and clothing.

WASHING

On the yarn label, you will generally find guidelines for washing your crocheted piece. These recommendations are based on the fibers that the yarn is made of.

Crochet pieces made with 100% cotton or linen can be washed by hand or using the delicate cycle of a washing machine with a detergent designed for delicate clothes. Before placing your pieces in the washing machine, slide them into a lingerie bag in order to avoid rubbing against other articles of clothing. After washing, lay the piece flat and away from any heat source in order to dry.

For crocheted pieces made out of 100% wool, silk, or viscose, it is preferable to hand wash them with cold water and a gentle detergent. However, your washing machine may have a special wool or delicate setting, which will ensure that the garment will be thoroughly cleaned. If you choose to machine wash, you should definitely choose the setting for cold water without spinning. When the washing machine has finished, wrap the piece in a towel without twisting too much. Lay the piece flat and away from any heat source.

The surface of wool fibers is composed of scales. The scales' reaction to temperature changes is what shrinks wool. This is why you must always wash wool pieces in cold water, so that you do not run the risk of them shrinking and felting.

Wash crocheted pieces made with natural and synthetic blends the same way you would wash wool. Even though synthetic fibers are more resistant to machine washing, it is preferable to not take risks and to avoid an accidental felting.

IRONING

Crocheted pieces made out of 100% wool and/or wool mixed with synthetic fibers do not need to be ironed if they have been dried flat. If their appearance is not impeccable, however, you can you may press them lightly.

Place a heavy cloth or several layers of finer cloths on the ironing board. Adjust the heat setting on the iron to the wool setting, without steam. Position a piece of dry, white, cotton cloth between the iron and the surface of the work (this trick prevents creating a sheen on the surface of the wool) and iron lightly in order to avoid leaving marks on your piece. Proceed in the same manner for silk and viscose but with the heat adjusted to the silk setting.

For the pieces made out of 100% cotton or linen, iron in the same way but select the setting for cotton and use a damp cloth as a press cloth. Shape the piece if necessary: pin it to the sheet to the desired dimensions and iron; the piece will then stretch and reshape. Wait for the piece to completely cool before taking out the pins.

Washing		This symbol is the symbol for washing. The numbers inside indicate at what temperature to wash it. The hand means that one should only wash it by hand. For example: 40°
Bleach		This symbol permits bleach with all types of products, chlorine or oxygen-based.
Drying		This symbol recommends the temperature to machine dry. 1 dot (.) = moderate temperature. 2 dots (..) = no restrictions. For example:
Ironing		This symbol defines the temperature to iron. 1 dot (.) = 110°. 2 dots (..) = 150°. 3 dots (...) = 200°. Example:
Dry cleaning		This symbol specifies that the piece should be dry cleaned.
Crossed symbols		A crossed symbol means not to wash or iron. For example:

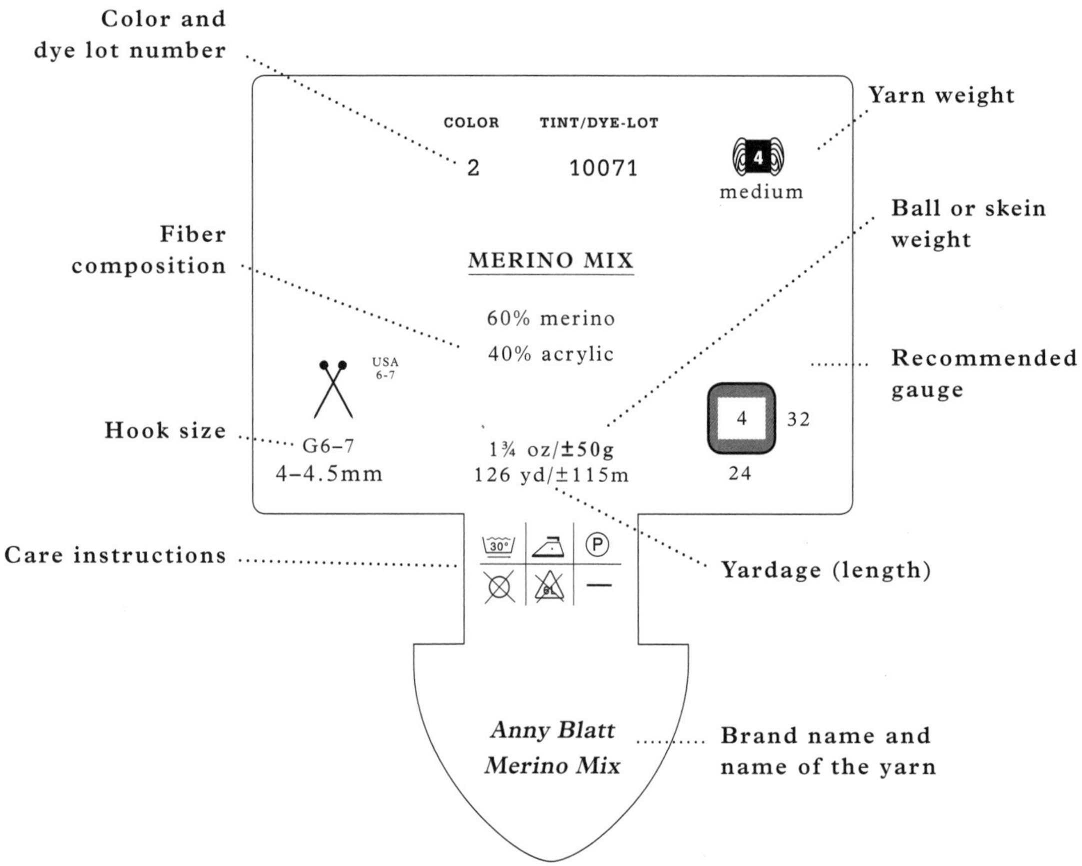

Color and dye lot number

COLOR 2

TINT/DYE-LOT 10071

Yarn weight

4 medium

Fiber composition

MERINO MIX

60% merino
40% acrylic

Ball or skein weight

USA 6-7

Recommended gauge

Hook size

G6–7
4–4.5mm

1¾ oz/±50g
126 yd/±115m

4 32
24

Care instructions

30°

Yardage (length)

Anny Blatt
Merino Mix

Brand name and name of the yarn

READING A LABEL

Yarn is sold in skeins or balls that always include a label. The labels provide essential guidance on what you should take into account when buying yarn.

The brand name and type of yarn: Manufacturers might produce this type of yarn from one season to the next or they may only produce it for a limited time. You should buy the necessary number of skeins to make your project to ensure that you will have enough yarn available to finish it.

The color and dye lot: This information is extremely important, especially if you need to buy additional skeins in order to finish your piece. A change in dye lot mid-project is very noticeable and unattractive.

The ball or skein weight: The weight depends on the composition of the yarn. You will generally find yarn produced in skeins weighing 25g or 30g for finer or more delicate yarns like silk, fine mohair, angora, or cashmere. Yarn is most often packaged in 1¾ oz (50g) balls, while balls and skeins of 3½ oz (100g) are reserved for thicker yarns.

Yardage: A fine yarn offers more yardage for the same weight of a thicker yarn. Thus, in order to make the same piece, a finer yarn can be more cost-efficient than a thicker yarn.

Hook size: You will often find a recommended size knitting needle printed on the label. Certain brands also include which hook size to use. If this suggestion is missing, you can refer to the needle size and convert the number to a hook size based on the mm measurements to make a swatch.

The swatch: Gauge is often specified by the number of stitches and rows based on a swatch knitted in stockinette stitch that is 4 inches square (10×10 cm). As with hook size, the swatch is essential in calculating gauge.

The composition: This information is required. Fiber content is indicated by the percentage of materials that make up the content of the yarn.

Care instructions: They are not obligatory but the manufacturers often give suggestions. Their recommendations are provided in the form of international symbols also used by the garment industry (page 17).

GAUGE

Before starting a project
Crocheting a swatch is essential. The yarn manufacturers' suggestions for the swatch are shown on the ball bands, but you must pay attention. Generally these are given for a knit project. You will not always find suggestions for a crochet swatch. However, this gives you an idea of the hook size to use, and you will adjust the number when you crochet a swatch.

Which size, which yarn, which stitch?
The swatch is most often a square measuring 4 inches (10cm) for fine to medium yarns. For thicker yarns, do not hesitate to make a swatch 8 inches (20cm) or even larger in order to check that the stitch and yarn combination corresponds to the gauge you expect. To determine the number of stitches necessary to crochet 4 inches (10cm) wide and to the number of rows to get 4 inches (10cm) high, you will count the number of chain stitches made at the beginning of the swatch and the number of rows crocheted to achieve the desired height. These dimensions can differ from the directions given in the pattern. You should therefore adapt these directions to your own gauge.

The swatch should be made in the stitch that will be used in the project to confirm that your choice of yarn looks good in this stitch, the hook size, and the chosen pattern. Finally, this exercise is the first experience with a new yarn, so use it to adjust to the correct tension based on the nature of the stitch pattern. Tension is different from one crocheter to another. If the stitch seems very loose and not very even, you should choose a smaller hook size. If the stitch looks very stiff and tight, change the hook size to one with a larger number, or go up two sizes if necessary.

A bit of calculation
Once the swatch is 4 inches (10cm) square, count the number of stitches along the width of the square and the number of rows along the height of it. If you have made a swatch of 8 inches (20cm) or more, draw a square of 4 inches (10cm) on a piece of light cardboard and cut it out. Lay the swatch flat and place the window on top, the bottom edge parallel to the foundation chain, then count the number of stitches along the width and height. In order to get the number of stitches per inch (or centimeter), divide the number of stitches in your swatch by 4 (10) and multiply the result by the number of inches (centimeters) indicated in the pattern. Repeat these calculations to get the number of stitches per row. If the pattern has several different stitch patterns, you should make a swatch for each stitch. If your pattern calls for colorwork, you should practice that in a swatch as well.

Other uses for gauge swatches

The swatch is also useful to see how the yarn holds up in the wash. Slide it into a lingerie bag and wash it in the machine on the wool or delicate setting, or in cold water if your machine lacks those options. Allow it to dry flat, then iron it lightly, placing a dry sheet between the swatch and the iron. Next, take the measurements and, if you notice any shrinkage, take that into account when making the final product. Check to make sure the colors have not bled or faded. If that is the case, you will need to fix the colors before the first washing. To do that, prepare a bath of 2½ gallons (10 liters) of cold water, adding 10 tablespoons of vinegar. Wet the crocheted piece in cold water before placing it in the bath. Let it sit for an hour and rinse it in cold water.

A little trick

Once you have finished your project, save the swatch. Place a label in a corner where you can indicate the type of yarn, the brand, the name of the stitch, and the size of the hook that you used. Keep these swatches easily accessible; they are very useful to help you remember the look of a stitch and the feel of a particular yarn. Also, if you need to repair the project in the future, you will have some of the yarn available for mending.

WHICH SIZE, WHICH YARN, WHICH CROCHET HOOK?

Yarn weight symbol & category names	Types of yarn in category	Crochet gauge* ranges in single crochet to 4"	Recommended hook in metric size range	Recommended hook in U.S. size range
0 Lace	10-count crochet thread	32–42 double crochets**	Steel** 1.6–1.4mm	Steel*** 6, 7, 8, regular hook B-1
1 Super Fine	Sock, Fingering, Baby	21–32 sts	2.25–3.5mm	B-1 to E-4
2 Fine	Sport, Baby	16–20 sts	3.5–4.5mm	E-4 to 7
3 Light	DK, Light Worsted	12–17 sts	4.5–5.5mm	7 to I-9
4 Medium	Worsted, Afghan, Aran	11–14 sts	5.5–6.5mm	I-9 to K-10½
5 Bulky	Chunky, Craft, Rug	8–11 sts	6.5–9mm	K-10½ to M-13
6 Super Bulky	Bulky, Roving	5–9 sts	9mm and larger	M-15 and larger

* Guidelines Only: The above reflect the most commonly used gauges and hook sizes for specific yarn categories.
** Lace weight yarns are usually crocheted on larger hooks to create lacey, openwork patterns. Accordingly, a gauge range is difficult to determine. Always follow the gauge stated in your pattern.
*** Steel crochet hooks are sized differently from regular hooks—the higher the number, the smaller the hook, which is the reverse of regular hook sizing.
(Source: Craft Yarn Council of America, www.YarnStandards.com)

TAKUMI K 6.5mm CLOVER
TAKUMI J 6.0mm CLOVER
NO.0 NO.2

HOOKS

The hook is the only tool you need to make all of the basic stitches (both plain and textured), to make lace, work in the round, and more. It is a simple tool, light and very portable, which you can easily slide into a bag and use anywhere you have a spare moment of time. Crochet is the perfect on-the-go activity.

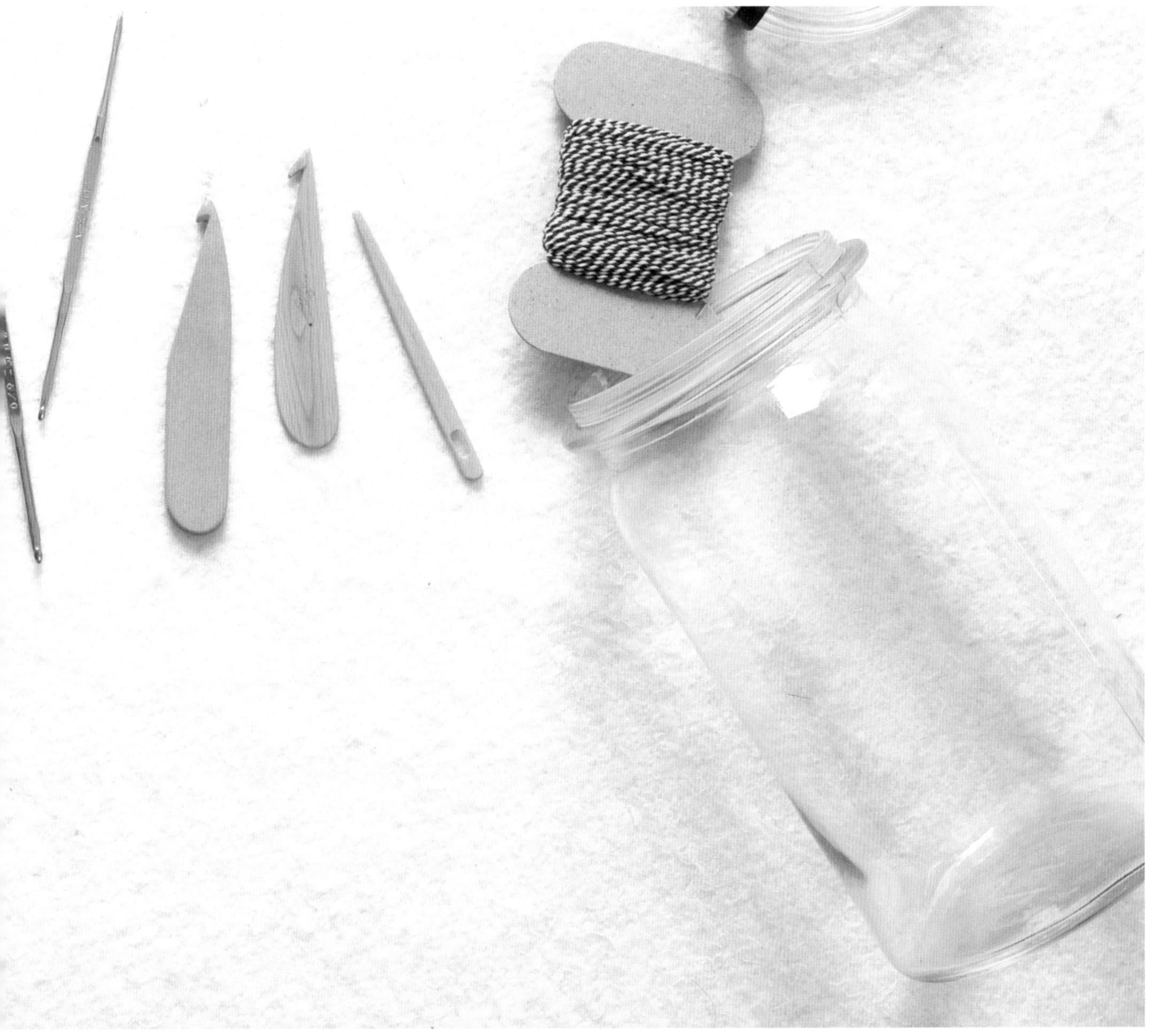

Crochet hooks come in a range of sizes, are made in different materials, and have unique uses and characteristics.

Hooks for fine and very fine yarns, which undergo a lot of stress while being worked, are made out of metal; the better quality ones are made out of steel. They have a very fine shaft and a flat surface on the first third of the handle for a better grip.

Crochet hooks made out of wood, bamboo, aluminum, or plastic are used for yarns of medium thickness. They can have an ergonomic handle so your fingers don't tense up while crocheting. Hooks made out of wood or bamboo are particularly useful for silk, rayon, or other very slippery fibers. Novelty yarns with an irregular surface are worked more easily with hooks made out of metal or plastic.

Finally, heavier yarns require larger plastic hooks to allow for the yarn's bulk. The body of these hooks often has a round handle without a flat surface to place your fingers.

Always choose the best tools you can find and afford. The end of the hook, thinner than the handle, should be very smooth without any bumps in order to avoid snagging the yarn. The shaft (or handle) should be very straight. If you have an old hook in your crocheting box or if you find one in a flea market, get rid of those that are rounded or bent. They will not be of any use to you. In fact, they might even damage the surface of the yarn, and the stitches will not be regular.

Store your crochet hooks in a case reserved for this purpose and have at your disposal a large range of hooks in different materials and of different sizes in order to be able to choose a hook best suited for the project and for the yarn. Hooks made out of bamboo are fragile, especially the finer ones, and plastic or wood hooks sometimes break if under a lot of pressure.

There is another type of crochet hook, which is longer and has a hook on both ends. This hook is only used for "Tunisian" crochet, a specialized technique that's different from the crochet techniques presented in this book.

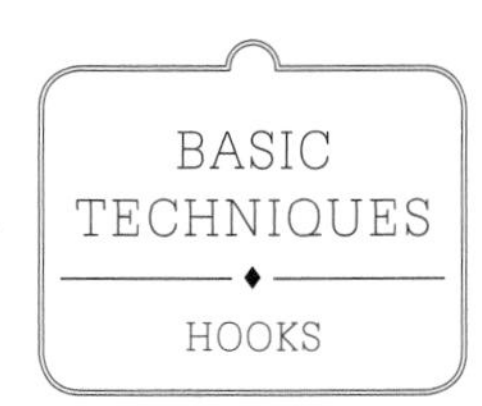

NUMBERING SYSTEM OF CROCHET HOOK SIZES

U.S. size	metric size	UK/Canadian size
B-1	2.25mm	12
C-2	2.75mm	11
D-3	3.25mm	10
E-4	3.5mm	9
F-5	3.75mm	8
G-6	4mm	7
7	4.5mm	—
H-8	5mm	6
I-9	5.5mm	5
J-10	6mm	4
K-10½	6.5mm	2
L-11	8mm	—
M/N-13	9mm	—
N/P-15	10mm	—
P/Q	15mm	—
Q	16mm	—
S	19mm	—

Leather handles
Felt balls
Sewing thread and
embroidery floss
Braided leather
handles
Beads in
different colors
Small notions box (1 pair of scissors, some pins,
yarn needles of different sizes)

NOTIONS

Besides a crochet hook, you will need a few other supplies to finish your projects. On these pages, you will find all the necessary notions needed to make the projects in this book. Additionally, I do recommend one good pair of scissors that you reserve only for your crocheted projects.

Pearlescent buttons

Buttons of various sizes

Novelty ribbon and leather trim

Faceted beads in various colors

THE VOCABULARY

Crochet uses some of the same terms as knitting, but also some specialized vocabulary words. In order to avoid really long patterns, these words are provided as abbreviations that generally correspond to the first two or three letters of the word.

Another type of explanation in crochet consists of illustrating stitches with symbols. Each symbol in a diagram corresponds to a type of stitch. The symbols come from an international nomenclature and are roughly identical throughout the world. This type of explanation also avoids excessively long written patterns and makes them easier to understand.

In order to better comprehend this vocabulary and these abbreviations as well as feel comfortable using diagrams, you must learn them and use them as soon as you begin to crochet. There are relatively few that you need to learn, and they are fairly logical.

ABBREVIATIONS

When you first look at the patterns, the instructions may seem like a secret, incomprehensible code. However, with a bit of attention, you will quickly learn how to decipher them. For your reference, here are the most commonly used abbreviations.

ndl = needle	yo = yarn over
inc = increase	st = stitch
dctog = double crochet together	ins = insert
ea = each	prev = previous
cont = continue	rep = repeat
sh = shell	rem = remaining
dec = decrease	nxt = next
tog = together	lp = loop

In this book, the beginning of each row is in bold, which allows you to easily keep your place in the pattern while crocheting.

THE SYMBOLS

In crochet diagrams, each stitch is illustrated with a symbol. You will find these symbols in every crochet pattern. They offer a visual explanation of the stitches used in a project.

Abbreviations and symbols for the stitches you'll find in the diagrams.

○ = **chain stitch** (ch)

● = **slip stitch** (sl st): Insert the crochet hook into 1 stitch, yarn over and pull it through the stitch and the loop that is on the hook.

X or + = **single crochet** (sc): Insert the crochet hook into 1 stitch, yarn over and pull it through the stitch. Yarn over and pull the yarn through the two loops on the hook.

X̲ = **back loop single crochet**: Work the first row with single crochets. Ch 1 to turn. Then, for the second row, single crochet by using the strand behind each stitch: insert the hook under the back loop of the stitch of the previous row, yarn over and pull it through the stitch. There are 2 loops on the hook. Yarn over, pull the yarn through the two loops on the hook—1 loop remains on the hook. Continue in the same way throughout the row.

T = **half-double crochet** (hdc): Yarn over, insert the hook into 1 stitch, yarn over, and pull it through the stitch, yarn over, and pull the yarn through the 3 loops on the hook.

Ŧ = **double crochet** (dc): Yarn over, insert the hook into 1 stitch, yarn over and pull it through the stitch. Yarn over again, pass the yarn through the 2 loops on the hook, yarn over, and pull the yarn through the last 2 loops on the hook.

Ŧ = **treble (or triple) crochet** (tc): Yarn over twice, insert the hook into a stitch, yarn over and pull it through the stitch, yarn over again, and pull the yarn through the first two loops on the hook. Yarn over again and pull the yarn through the next 2 loops on the hook, yarn over, and pull the yarn through the last 2 loops on the hook.

= **front post double crochet**: Yarn over, insert the crochet hook horizontally, from right to left, under the post of the stitch from the previous row, yarn over and bring it through the stitch. Yarn over again, pass the yarn through the first 2 stitches on the crochet hook, yarn over, and pull the yarn through the last 2 stitches on the crochet hook.

= **2 double crochets worked together** (dc2tog or 2 st bobble): Yarn over, insert the crochet hook into 1 stitch, yarn over and pull it through the stitch, yarn over, and pull the yarn through the first 2 loops—2 loops remain on the crochet hook. Yarn over, insert the crochet hook into the same (or next) stitch, yarn over, pull it through the stitch, yarn over and pull it through the 3 loops on the hook. In order to make this stitch, depending on the desired effect, one inserts the crochet hook into the same stitch (for a bobble) or in consecutive stitches (for a dc2tog). It will be indicated in the pattern notes.

= **3 double crochets worked together** (dc3tog or 3 st bobble): Yarn over, insert the crochet hook into 1 stitch, yarn over, pull the yarn through the stitch, yarn over, and pull the yarn through the first 2 loops on the hook—2 loops remain on the hook. Yarn over, insert the hook into the same (or next) stitch, yarn over, pull it through the stitch, yarn over, and pull the yarn through the first two loops—3 loops remain on the hook. Yarn over, insert the hook into the same (or next) stitch, yarn over, pull it through the stitch, yarn over, and pull the yarn through the first 2 loops on the hook—4 loops remain on the hook. Yarn over and pull the yarn through all 4 loops on the crochet hook. In order to make this stitch, depending on the desired effect, insert the hook into the same stitch (for a bobble) or in consecutive stitches (for a dc3tog). It will be indicated in the pattern notes.

= **4 double crochets worked together** (dc4tog or 4 st bobble): Yarn over, insert the crochet hook into 1 stitch, yarn over, pull the yarn through the stitch, yarn over, and pull the yarn through the first 2 loops on the hook—2 loops remain on the hook. Yarn over, insert the hook into the same (or next) stitch, yarn over, pull it through the stitch, yarn over, and pull the yarn through the first two loops—3 loops remain on the hook. Yarn over, insert the hook into the same (or next) stitch, yarn over, pull it through the stitch, yarn over, and pull the yarn through the first 2 loops on the hook—4 loops remain on the hook. Yarn over, insert the hook into the same (or next) stitch, yarn over, pull the yarn through the stitch, yarn over, and pull the yarn through the first 2 loops on the hook—5 loops remain on the hook. Yarn over one last time and pull it through all 5 loops on the crochet hook. In order to make this stitch, depending on the desired effect, one inserts the hook into the same stitch (for a bobble) or in consecutive stitches (for a dc4tog). It will be indicated in the pattern notes.

= **5 double crochets worked together** (dc5tog or 5 st bobble): Yarn over, insert the crochet hook in 1 stitch, yarn over, pull the yarn through the stitch, yarn over, pull the yarn through the first 2 loops on the hook, 2 loops remain on the hook. Yarn over, insert the hook into the same (or next) stitch, yarn over, pull it through the stitch, yarn over, pull the yarn through the first two loops, 3 loops remain on the hook. Yarn over, insert the hook into the same (or next) stitch, yarn over, pull it through the stitch, yarn over, and pull the yarn through the first 2 loops on the hook—4 loops remain on the hook. Yarn over, insert the hook into the same (or next) stitch, yarn over, pull the yarn through the stitch, yarn over, and pass the yarn through the first 2 loops on the hook—5 loops remain on the hook. Yarn over, insert the hook into the same (or next) stitch, yarn over, pull the yarn through the stitch, yarn over, and pull the yarn through the first 2 loops—6 loops remain on the hook. Yarn over one last time and pull it through all 6 loops on the crochet hook. In order to make this stitch, depending on the desired effect, one inserts the hook into the same stitch (for a bobble) or in consecutive stitches (for a dc5tog). It will be indicated in the pattern notes.

= **puff**: Yarn over, insert the crochet hook into 1 stitch, yarn over, and pull the yarn through the stitch, making sure the stitches are loose. There are 3 loops on the hook. Yarn over, insert the hook into the same stitch, yarn over, and pull it through the stitch, keeping stitches loose. There are 5 loops on the hook. Yarn over, insert the hook into the same stitch, yarn over, and pull it through the stitch, keeping stitches loose. There are 7 loops on the hook. Yarn over, insert the stitch into the same stitch, yarn over, and pull it through the stitch, keeping stitches loose. There are 9 loops on the hook. Yarn over, insert the hook into the same stitch, yarn over, and pull it through the stitch, keeping stitches loose. There are 11 loops on the hook. Yarn over, and pull it through all 11 loops. Yarn over one last time and pull it through the last loop on the crochet hook. A puff can be composed of several half double crochets; the number will be indicated in the pattern notes.

= **picot** (pic) of 3 chain stitches: Chain 3 stitches, single crochet (or slip stitch) in the first of these 3 stitches. A picot can be composed of several chain stitches; the number will be indicated in the pattern notes.

THE FIRST STITCH

1/ holding the yarn and the crochet hook

Hold the crochet hook in the right hand as if it were a pencil, with the tip pointing towards the bottom, the thumb and the index finger placed on either side of the flattened surface on the handle.

2/ make the first stitch

1 Make a loop.

2 Insert the hook into this loop.

3 Catch the yarn attached to the ball with the hook (= 1 yarn over).

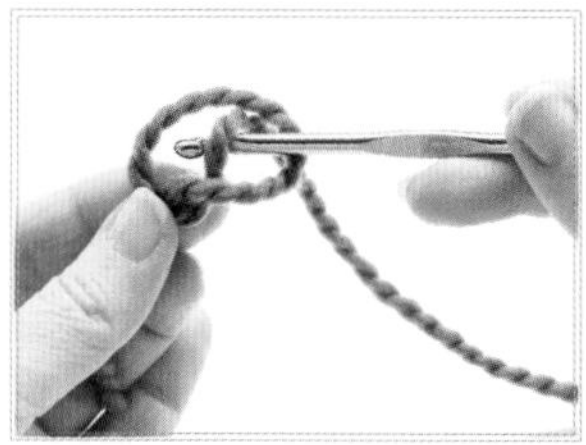

4 Pull the yarn attached to the ball through this loop.

5 Tighten the loop on the hook and place the knot on the hook.

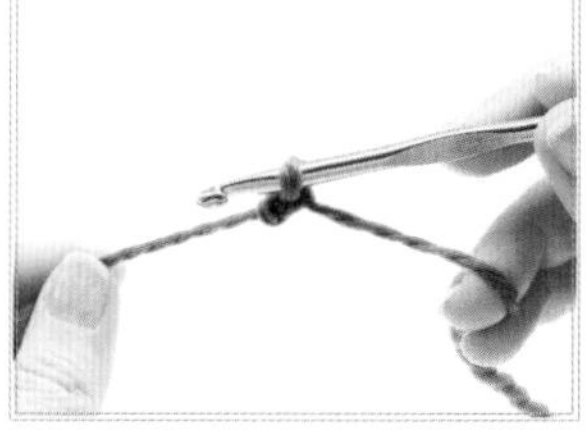

6 Place the yarn attached to the ball in the left hand and control the tension by sliding the strand between the index finger and the pinkie.

For left-handed people, proceed in the same way holding the crochet hook in the left hand and the working yarn in the right hand. Left-handed people can follow the directions in this book given for right-handed people by placing a mirror along the pictures instead of inverting the directions. The written directions and the symbols are identical for left-handed people and right-handed people.

STARTING AND ENDING A ROW

At the beginning of each row and depending on the nature of the stitch, you must make a certain number of chain stitches. This number of stitches corresponds to the height that the row will attain while working the pattern stitch. It is generally indicated in the pattern. This or these chain stitches at the beginning replace the first stitch of the row.

The table below gives guidelines for beginning the row with the correct turning chain.

Type of crochet stitch in the row	Number of chain stitch(es) to make	For the first stitch after the turning chain, insert hook in the _____ stitch from end.
Single crochet	1	Second
Half-double crochet	2	Third
Double crochet	3	Fourth
Treble crochet	4	Fifth

In order to finish the row flawlessly, the last stitch should be worked in the first chain stitch from the beginning of the previous row (if you have made a single crochet) or in the second chain stitch when you have made several to make a row of half-double, double, or treble crochets. The schematics on the opposite page will help you make the first and the last stitch of the row correctly. With these four methods, the edges of your crocheted piece will turn out straight.

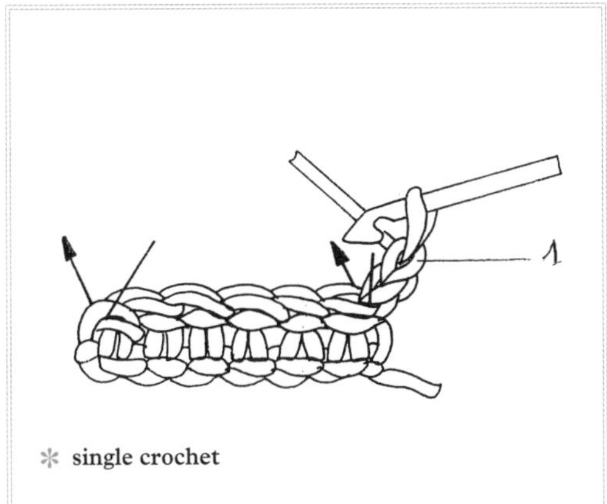

✱ single crochet

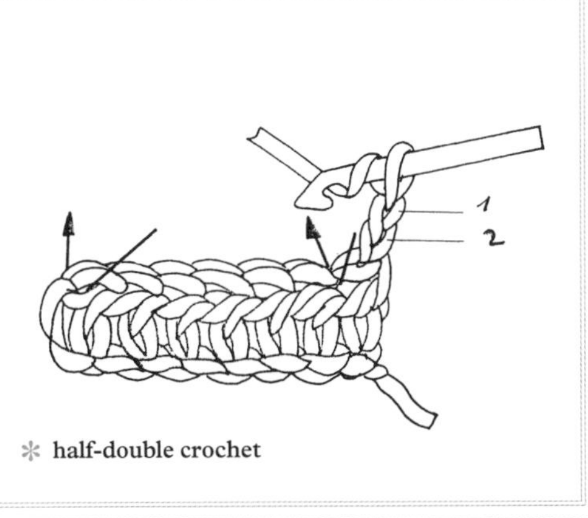

✱ half-double crochet

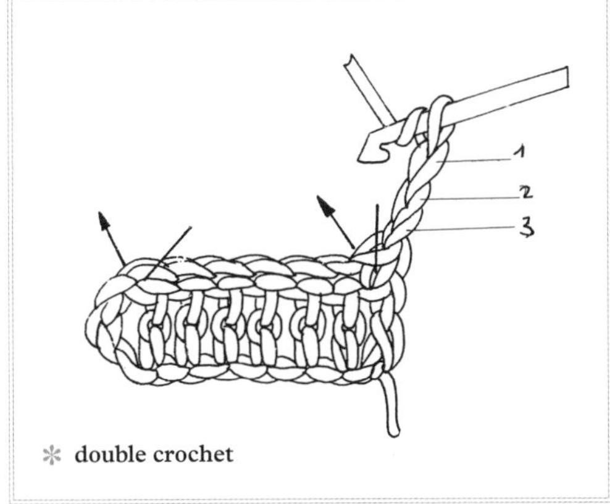

✱ double crochet

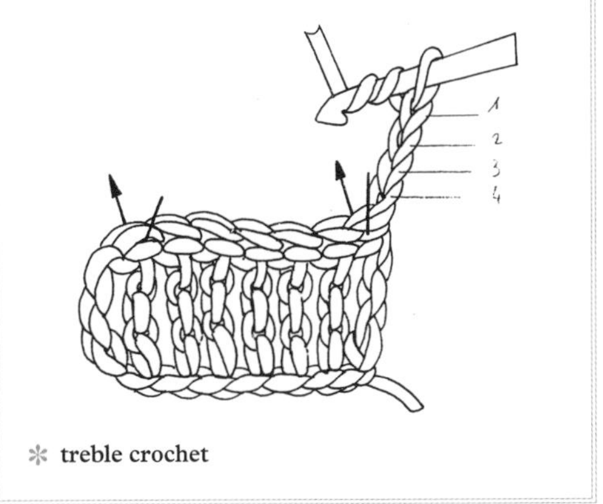

✱ treble crochet

CHAPTER 1

MASTERING THE 6 ESSENTIAL STITCHES

CHAPTER 1

lesson 1

MASTERING THE 6 ESSENTIAL STITCHES

LESSON 1

CHAIN STITCH

project: make a necklace*

directions → pages 44–45 • assembly → page 45 • stitch page → 76

MATERIALS

5 skeins fingering weight yarn, 51% pure wool, 49% kid mohair, 280 yd (255m), 1¾ oz (50g), 1 skein each in lilac, plum, grape, olive, and charcoal (1)

Size 5 (1.9mm) steel crochet hook

Approximately 60 faceted seed beads in iridescent green, silver, and amber

1 flat metal ring

Yarn needle

Scissors

Straight pins

STITCH USED

Chain stitch

SIZE

One size

GAUGE

25 stitches = 4" (10cm) long

DIMENSIONS

40¼" long, with clasp (102cm)

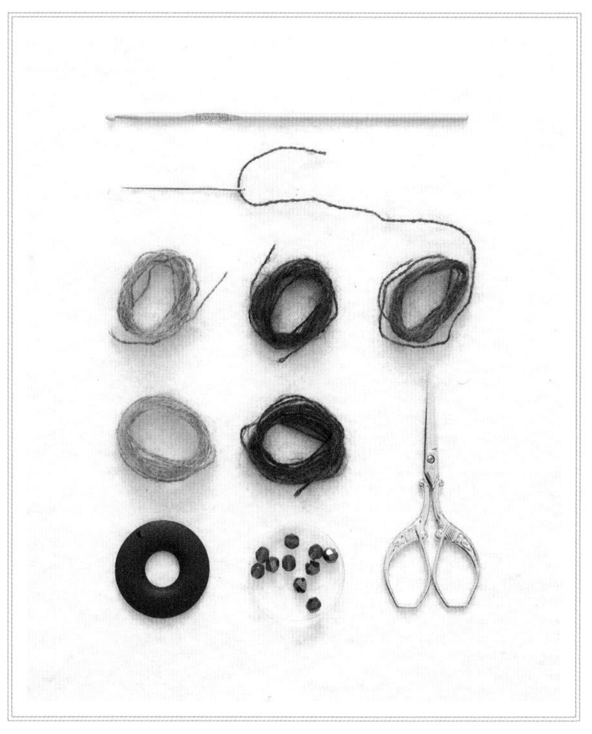

* Learn and practice creating a foundation chain, also called a base chain.

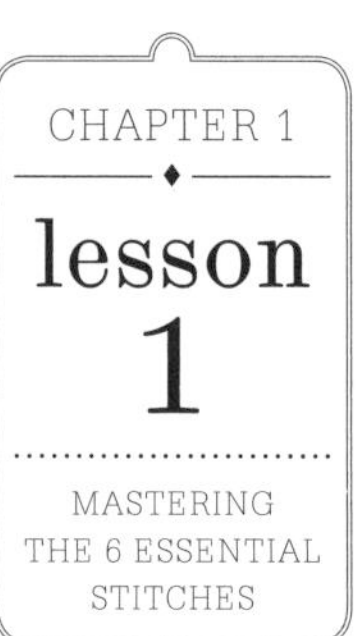

1/ learn the chain stitch (ch) ○

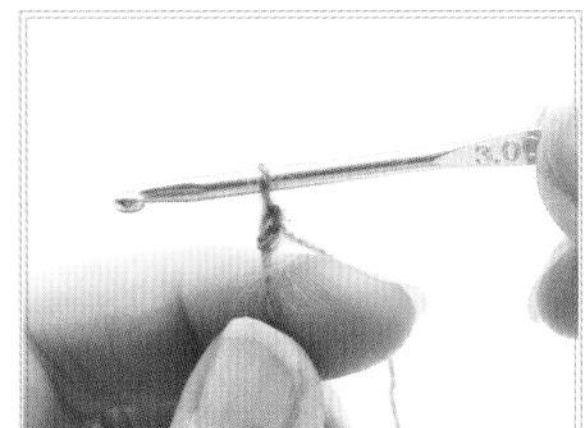

1 Place the slip knot on the index finger of the left hand, the tail placed in the palm of the hand.

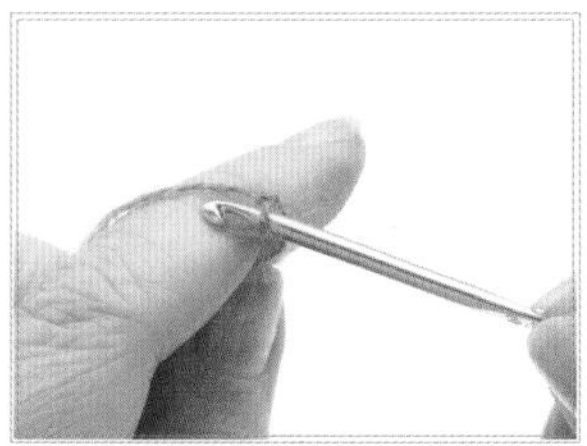

2 With the hook of the crochet hook, find the strand located behind the first stitch.

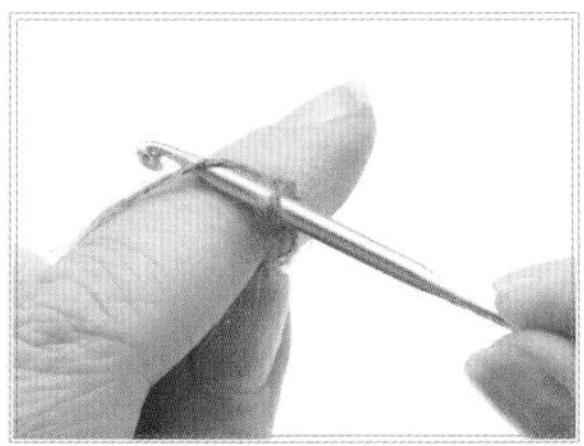

3 Yarn over and pass the head of the hook under the strand attached to the ball.

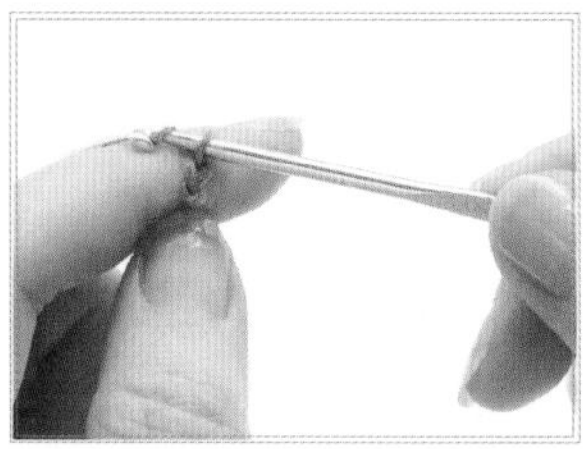

4 Pull the crochet hook toward the loop.

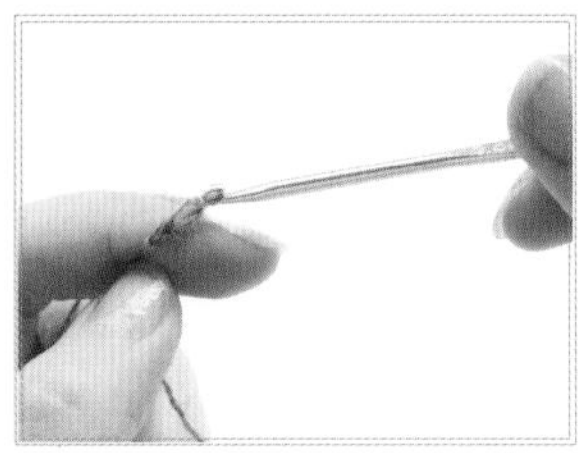

5 Pull the yarn over through the loop.

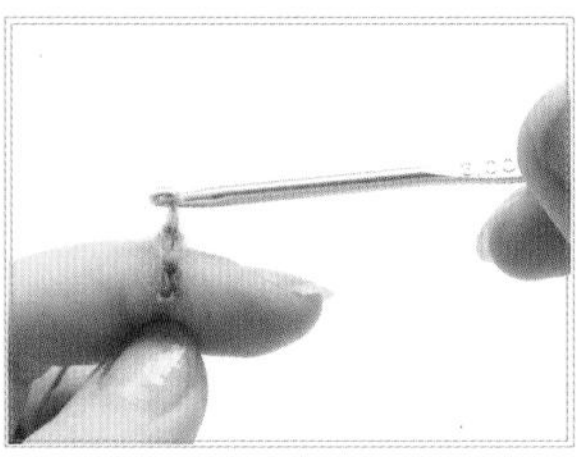

6 The first chain is formed.

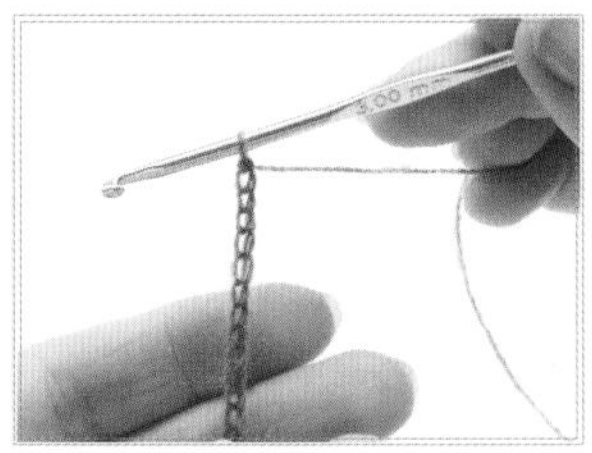

7 Continue in this way to make the number of chains indicated in the directions.

2/ make the necklace

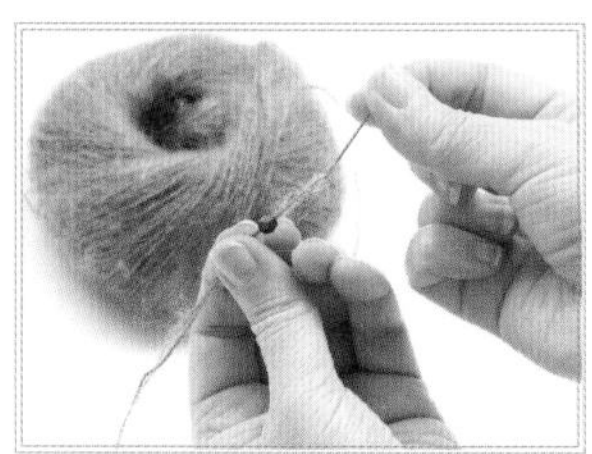

1 Insert the end of the yarn into the yarn needle.

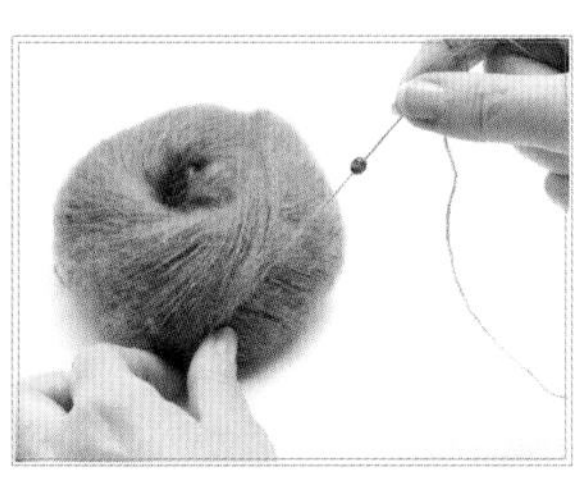

2 Slide 8–12 beads onto the yarn, randomly alternating colors according to the instructions opposite.

3 Leave 10" (25.5cm) of the yarn free at the beginning of the ball. Place the beads on each ball in this way.

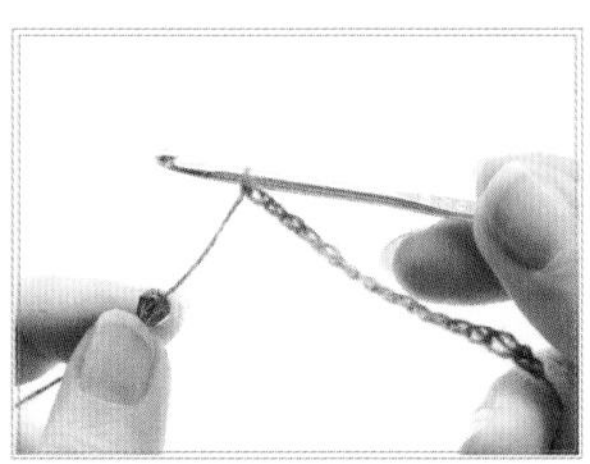

4 Make the chain while incorporating the beads: slide a bead up the yarn until it is at the level of the hook.

NECKLACE

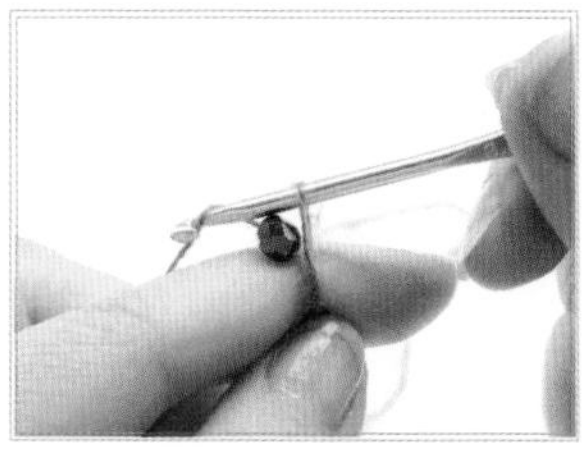

5 Yarn over, snagging the yarn behind the bead. Slide the yarn from the yarn over through the loop.

6 The bead is now enclosed in the chain. Continue the chain.

Charcoal strand
With the size 5 (1.9mm) crochet hook, make a chain as follows: ch 50 — 1 bead — ch 25 — 1 bead — ch 15 — 1 bead — ch 30 — 1 bead — ch 10 — 1 bead — ch 15 — 1 bead — ch 5 — 1 bead — ch 20 — 1 bead — ch 15 — 1 bead — ch 30 — 1 bead. Break the yarn, leaving 10" (25.5cm).

Plum strand
With the size 5 (1.9mm) crochet hook, make a chain as follows: ch 45 — 1 bead — ch 25 — 1 bead — ch 5 — 1 bead – ch 30 – 1 bead – ch 15 – 1 bead – ch 15 – 1 bead – ch 20 – 1 bead – ch 10 – 1 bead – ch 30 – 1 bead – ch 10 – 1 bead – ch 5 – 1 bead – ch 25. Break the yarn, leaving 10" (25.5cm).

Grape strand
With the size 5 (1.9mm) crochet hook, make a chain as follows: ch 45 – 1 bead – ch 30 – 1 bead – ch 15 – 1 bead – ch 5 – 1 bead – ch 20 – 1 bead – ch 20 – 1 bead – ch 15 – 1 bead – ch 10 – 1 bead – ch 30 – 1 bead – ch 10 – 1 bead – ch 45. Break the yarn, leaving 10" (25.5cm).

Olive strand
With the size 5 (1.9mm) crochet hook, make a chain as follows: ch 30 – 1 bead – ch 30 – 1 bead – ch 20 – 1 bead – ch 25 – 1 bead – ch 5 – 1 bead – ch 30 – 1 bead – ch 15 – 1 bead – ch 25 – 1 bead – ch 5. Break the yarn, leaving 10" (25.5cm).

Lilac strand
With the size 5 (1.9mm) crochet hook, make a chain as follows: ch 40 – 1 bead – ch 10 – 1 bead – ch 25 – 1 bead – ch 5 – 1 bead – ch 15 – 1 bead – ch 5 – 1 bead – ch 20 – 1 bead – ch 15 – 1 bead – ch 30 – 1 bead – ch 10 – 1 bead – ch 30 – 1 bead – ch 10 – 1 bead – ch 25. Break the yarn, leaving 10" (25.5cm).

3/ assemble the necklace

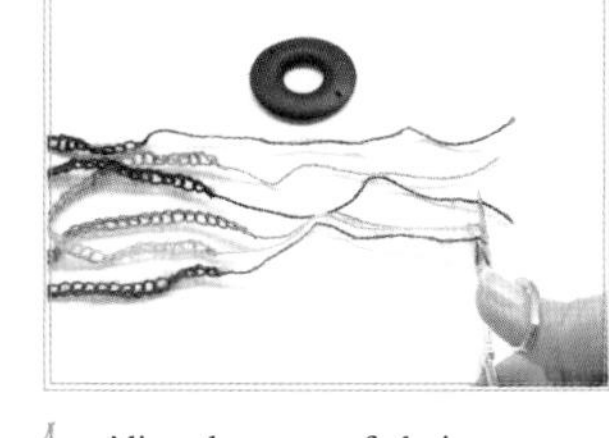

1 Align the rows of chains one next to the other. Even out the ends of the strands.

2 Pass the 6 strands through the hole of the ring.

3 Fold the strands in half. Insert the yarn needle through the base of the chains, wrapping the yarn several times around the base of the chains.

4 Finish by inserting the yarn needle twice underneath the wraps. Cut the yarn close to the necklace.

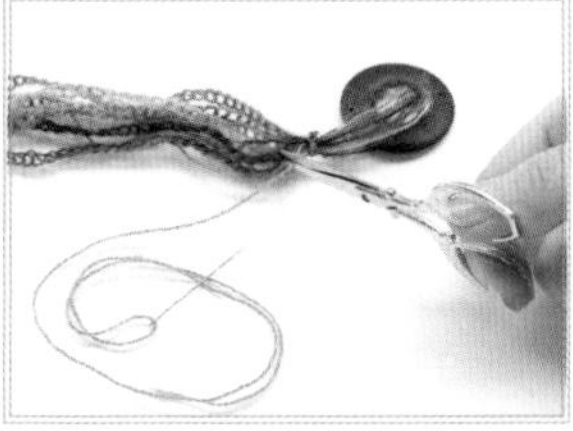

5 Repeat with the other end of the necklace, using the same ring.

CHAPTER 1

lesson 2

MASTERING THE 6 ESSENTIAL STITCHES

LESSON 2

SLIP STITCH

project: make a cloche hat*

directions → pages 48–49 • assembly → page 49 • stitch → page 77

MATERIALS

4 skeins of worsted weight yarn, 100% wool, 55 yd (50m), 1¾ (50g), 3 skeins in purple and 1 skein in gray (4)

Size H-8 (5mm) crochet hook

Yarn needle

Scissors

Straight pins

STITCH USED

Slip stitch

SIZE

One size

GAUGE

12 stitches = 4" (10 cm) wide

DIMENSIONS

22½ circumference without brim x 6¼ high (57cm x 17cm)

* You will also learn how to make a three-dimensional object with a simple crochet stitch in this lesson.

1/ the slip stitch (sl st) ●

→ **WORD OF ADVICE!**
Remember the abbreviation of the slip stitch, sl st, and its symbol.

1 Make the base chain.

2 In order to make the first row of the slip stitch, insert into the 2nd chain from the hook and yarn over.

3 Pull the yarn simultaneously through the stitch and the loop that is on the hook.

4 There will be only one loop on the hook.

5 Repeat the previous step in order to make the next slip stitch.

6 Finish the row by inserting the hook into the last st.

7 Yarn over.

8 Pull the yarn through the stitch and the loop that is on the hook.

2/ make the braid

→ **WORD OF ADVICE!**
This project might look very long, but don't panic. It is very easy.

With an H-8 (5mm) crochet hook, make a chain of 12 yd (11m). Ch 1 to turn, then sl st in each stitch from the chain.

3/ end the piece

→ **WORD OF ADVICE!**
Finishing instructions are indicated for every crochet pattern.

1 Cut the yarn 4" (10cm) from the work.

2 Open the last stitch, pull the cut strand through, and gently tug to tighten.

4/ sew the cloche hat

→ **WORD OF ADVICE! Coil the braid around itself in order to make the cloche hat, little by little.**

1 Thread a yarn needle with the same yarn. Fold the braid over 1¼" (3cm) from the end. Pin together.

2 Sew this folded piece at the slipped stitches at the bottom of the braid. That will be the inside of the hat.

3 Coil the crocheted braid in a spiral, and sew.

4 Continue coiling the braid in the same way and sew it at the slipped stitches as you go along.

5 At 22½" (57cm) circumference, continue the hat by placing the rows one under the other in order to make the height of the hat.

6 Secure with slipped stitches. At 6¾" (17cm) in height, continue by placing the rows parallel to each other to make the brim. Work for another 2" (5cm).

5/ add detail

→ **WORD OF ADVICE! The border is added with a blanket stitch in a contrasting color.**

1 Thread a yarn needle with contrasting yarn. Insert needle near the edge from underneath brim to the top. Insert needle to the right, ½" (13mm) in from the edge.

2 Slide the needle through the yarn loop and tighten smoothly to make the first stitch.

3 Continue as such for the entire circumference of the hat. End by making a little straight stitch.

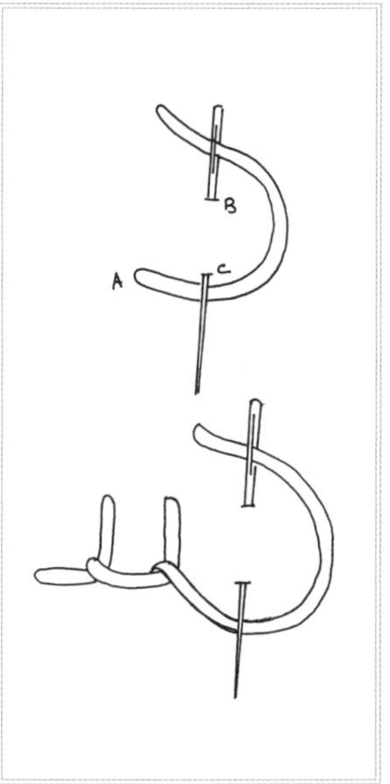

✻ **blanket stitch**

CHAPTER 1

lesson 3

MASTERING THE 6 ESSENTIAL STITCHES

LESSON 3

THE SLIP STITCH

project: make a little pouch*

directions → pages 52–54 • assembly → page 55 • stitch → page 77

MATERIALS

5 skeins of fingering weight yarn, 100% wool, 200 yd (180m), 1¾ (50g), 1 skein each in light blue, beige, lilac, and spring green (1)

Size B-1 (2.25mm) crochet hook

Yarn needle

4 small, pearlescent buttons

Scissors

Straight pins

STITCH USED

Single crochet

SIZE

One size

GAUGE

24 stitches = 4" (10cm) wide

30 rows = 4" (10cm) high

DIMENSIONS

3¼" wide x 4¼" high (8cm x 11cm) for little pouch

3¾" wide x 4¾" high (9.5cm x 12cm) for big pouch

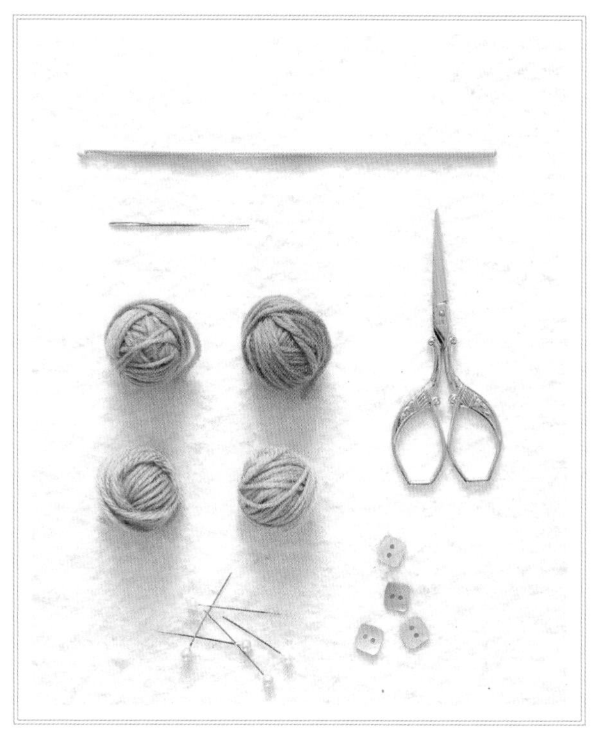

* You will also learn how to begin a new ball of yarn and change colors in this lesson.

1/ single crochet (sc)

X or +

→ **WORD OF ADVICE!**
Remember the abbreviation for single crochet, sc, and its symbol.

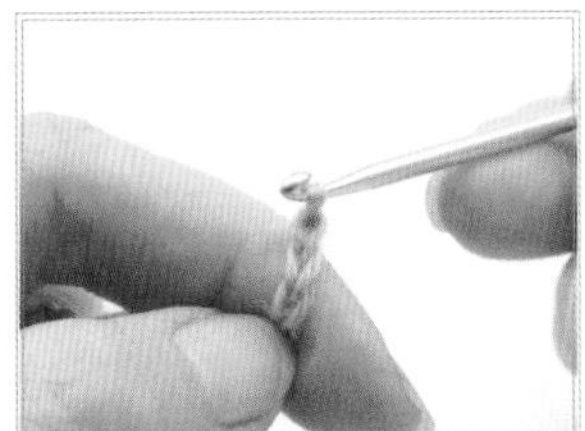

1 Make a foundation chain.

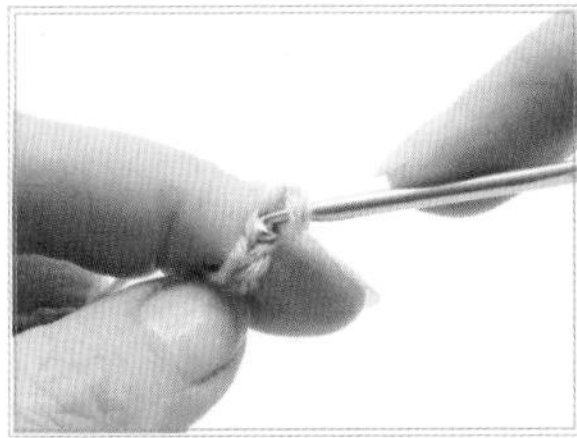

2 Insert the hook into the 2nd chain from the hook.

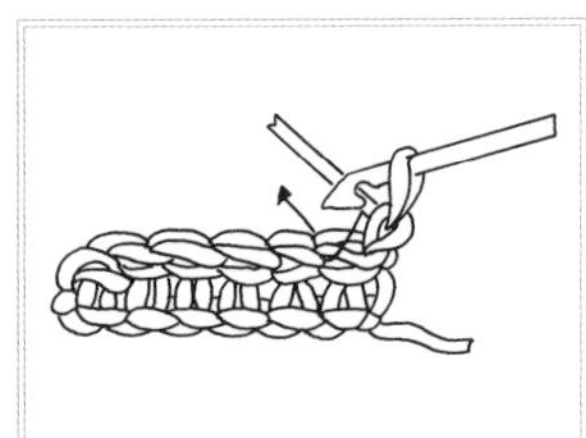

3 On the following rows, in order to turn, you will chain 1 and always begin the row from the 2nd stitch from the hook.

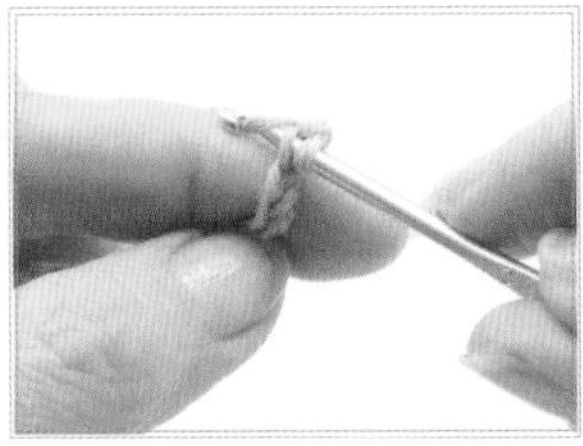

4 Yarn over by placing the hook under the strand still connected to the ball.

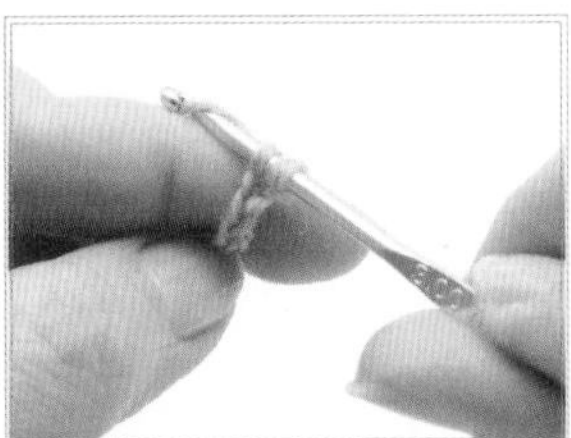

5 Pull the yarn over through the st. There are 2 loops on the hook. Yarn over and pull the yarn through the 2 loops. There is 1 loop on the hook.

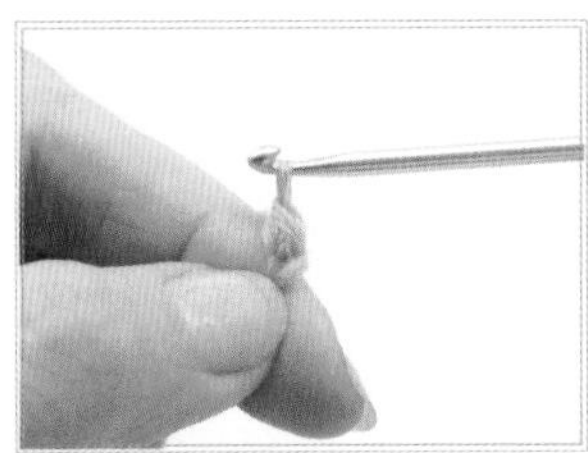

6 Insert hook into the next stitch and repeat steps 4 and 5 across.

7 At the end of the row, insert into the last stitch and sc 1.

8 Ch 1 and turn the fabric in order to work from right to left.

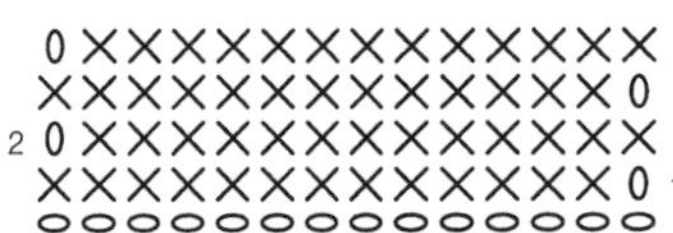

✻ **single crochet**

LITTLE POUCH

2/ change yarn

→ **WORD OF ADVICE!**
This technique is useful for all of the crochet stitches.

1 In order to change colors or start a new ball, catch the new yarn with the crochet hook.

2 Slide the strand of the new ball through the loop that is on the hook.

3 Continue working in sc.

3/ make a buttonhole

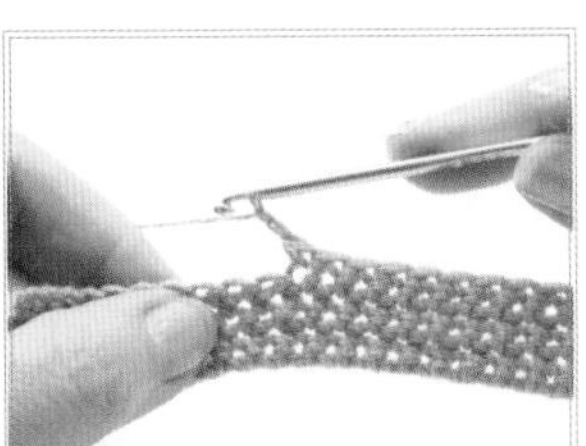

1 Ch 2.

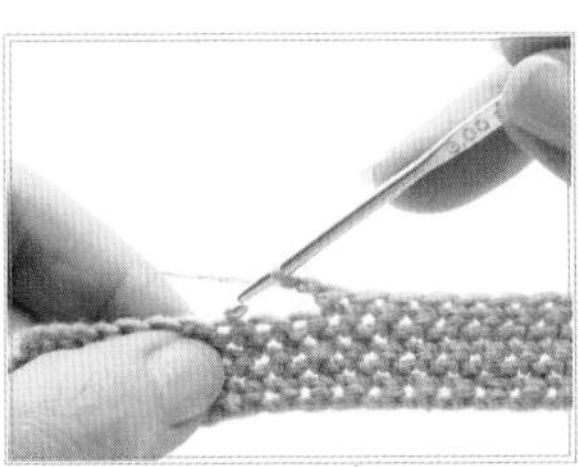

2 Skip 2 stitches and insert the hook into the 3rd stitch.

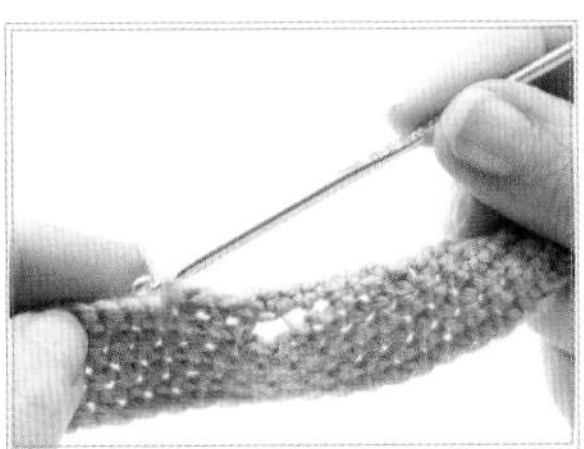

3 Continue in sc and finish the row.

4/ the little pouch

Base
With mauve, ch 50.
For rows 1–10: Ch 1 to turn, then sc across the row.
For rows 11 and 12: Using spring green, work 2 rows in sc.
For rows 13 and 14: Using beige, work 2 rows in sc.
For rows 15 and 16: Using light blue, work 2 rows in sc.
For rows 17–27: Switch back to mauve and continue in sc.
End the work at the end of row 27.

Flap
With mauve, ch 20.
For rows 1 and 2: Ch 1 to turn, then sc across the row.
For rows 3 and 4: Using spring green, work 2 rows in sc.
For rows 5 and 6: Using beige, work 2 rows in sc.
For row 7: Using light blue, work 1 row in sc.
For row 8: Using glacier, ch 1 to turn, sc 3, then make the first buttonhole: ch 2, skip 2 sts, insert the hook into the 3rd st. Continue in sc over the next 8 sts, ch 2, skip 2 sts, and end with sc over the last 4 sts.
For rows 9 and 10: Using mauve, work 2 rows in sc. On the 2 ch sts that make the buttonhole, sc in each ch st.
End the work at the end of row 10.

5/ the big pouch

Base
Using beige, ch 28.
For rows 1–13: Ch 1 to turn, then sc across the row.
For row 14: Ch 1 to turn, sc 10, switch to glacier and sc 7, switch back to beige and finish the row with 10 sc.
For rows 15 and 16: Ch 1 to turn, then sc across the row.
For row 17: Ch 1 to turn, sc 7, switch to glacier and sc 13, switch back to beige and finish the row with 7 sc.
For rows 18 and 19: Ch 1 to turn, then sc across the row.
For row 20: Work as for row 14.
For rows 21–46: Ch 1 to turn, then sc across the row.
For row 47: Work as for row 14.
For rows 48 and 49: Ch 1 to turn, then sc across the row.
For row 50: Work as for row 17.
For rows 51 and 52: Ch 1 to turn, then sc across the row.
For row 53: Work as for row 14.
For rows 54-67: Ch 1 to turn, then sc across the row.
End the work at the end of row 67.

Flap
Using light blue, ch 28.
Rows 1–7: Ch 1 to turn, then sc across the row.
Row 8: Ch 1 to turn, sc 5, then make the first buttonhole in the following way: ch 2, skip 2 sts, insert the hook into the 3rd st, sc in the next 12 sts. Make the second buttonhole: ch 2, skip 2 sts, and sc in the last 6 sts.
Rows 9 and 10: Work in sc for 2 rows. In the 2 ch sts that make the buttonhole, sc 1 in each ch st.
Finish the work at the end of row 10.

6/ sew the pouch

→ WORD OF ADVICE!
Pay attention to the two sides when sewing to create a neat appearance. The flap is sewn in the same way.

1 Fold the bottom right side against top right side.

2 Pin the piece with straight pins.

3 Sew a seam ¼" (5mm) from the edges.

4 Turn right side out and sew the buttons to line up with the buttonholes.

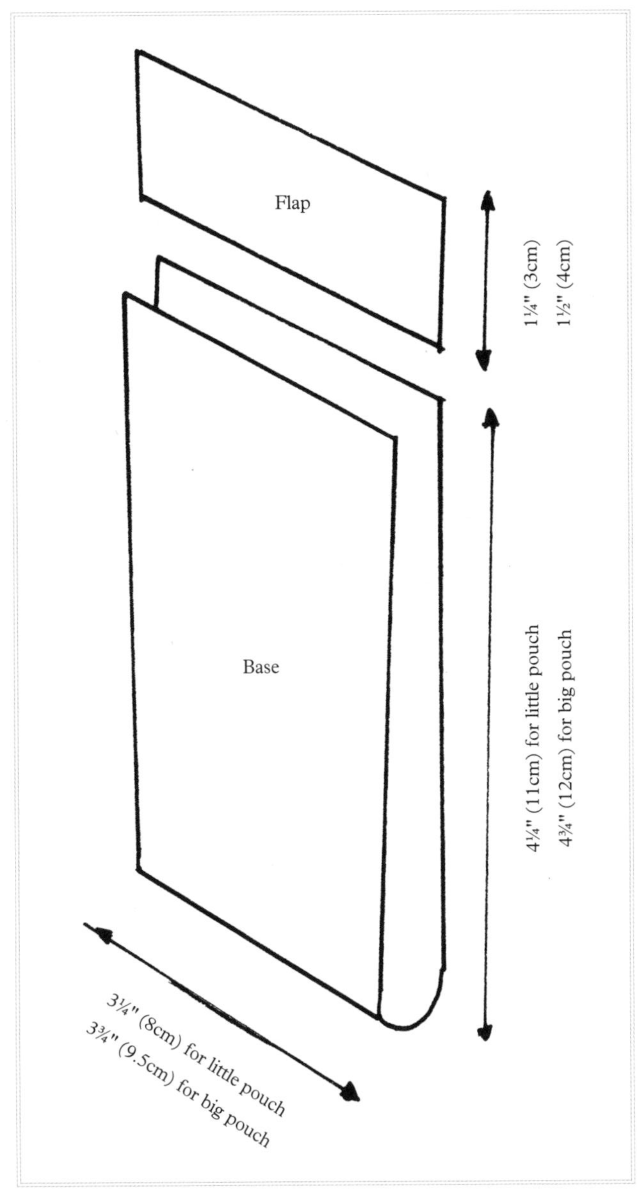

schematic for assembly

CHAPTER 1

lesson 4

MASTERING THE 6 ESSENTIAL STITCHES

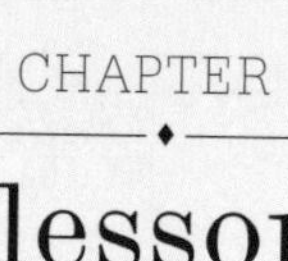

HALF-DOUBLE CROCHET

project 1: make a cowl*

directions → pages 58–59 • assembly → page 59 • variations → pages 60 and 62 • stitch → page 78

MATERIALS

10 skeins of worsted-weight yarn, 60% alpaca, 40% wool, 80 yd (75m), 1¾ (50g) in ecru (4)

Size N-15 (10mm) crochet hook

Yarn needle

Scissors

STITCH USED

Half-double crochet

SIZE

One size

GAUGE

7 stitches = 4" (10cm) wide

6 rows = 4" (10cm) high wide

DIMENSIONS

34½" circumference x 9¾" high (85cm x 25cm)

* In this lesson, you will also learn how to use a yarn needle to assemble a crocheted piece by grafting. Refer back to this lesson while crocheting your projects.

1/ half-double crochet (hdc)

→ **WORD OF ADVICE!**
Memorize this abbreviation, hdc, and symbol.

1 From the foundation chain, yarn over.

2 Insert the hook into the 3rd stitch.

3 Yarn over again.

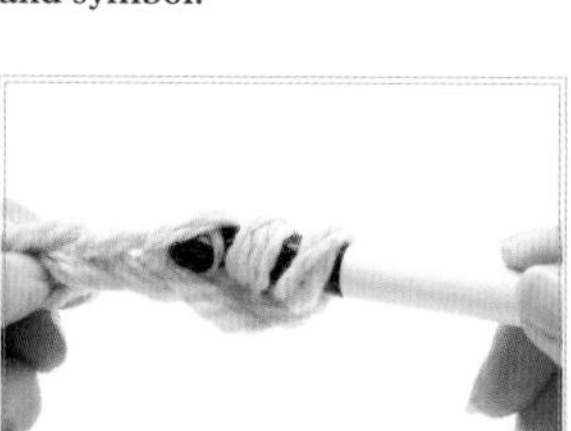

4 Pull the yarn through the stitch.

5 There are 3 loops on the hook.

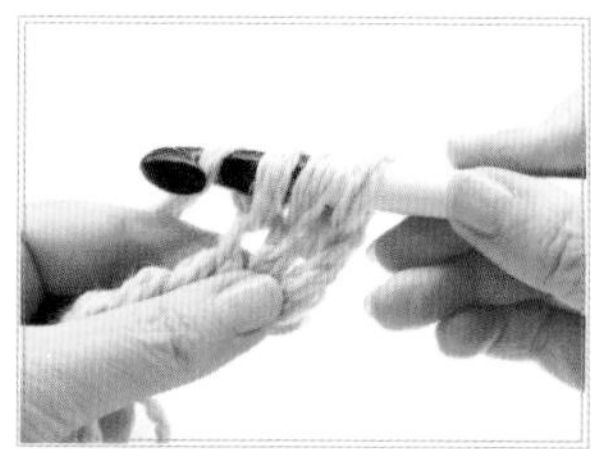

6 Yarn over again.

7 Pull the yarn through the 3 loops. There is 1 loop on the hook.

8 For the following hdc, yarnover 1, then insert into the next st.

9 Continue in the same way for the rest of the row.

10 At the end of the row, work the last half-double crochet in the last st from the beginning of the previous row.

11 Ch 2, then turn the work to begin a new row.

2/ make the cowl

Hold 4 strands of yarn together at the same time.
Ch 60 sts = 34½" (85cm).
To make the band, work 15 rows in hdc until 9¾" (25cm) high.
End after row 15.

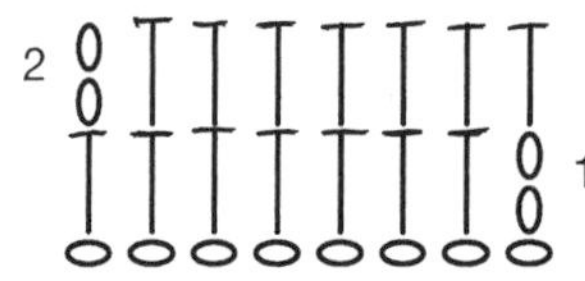

✻ **half-double crochet**

3/ weave in the ends

→ **WORD OF ADVICE!**
It's essential that you weave in the ends before starting to assemble the cowl.

1 Thread a yarn needle with the loose strands.

2 Weave the yarn through the edge stitches for at least 2" (5 cm).

3 Cut the remaining length of yarn close to the fabric.

4/ sew the cowl

→ **WORD OF ADVICE!**
This technique is called grafting. The seam is invisible and flat.

1 Thread a yarn needle with two strands of yarn. Place the two edges of the scarf side by side, right side facing you.

2 Slide the yarn needle through the fabric over 1" (2.5cm), then insert the needle back through close to the edge. Insert the needle from bottom to top on the left side of the scarf, ¼" (6mm) from the edge.

3 Gently tighten the stitch. Insert in the same way on the right edge, in the stitch above the first stitch.

4 Alternate a stitch on the right with a stitch on the left, at regular intervals, going up the length of the edges of the piece.

5 Gently tighten the stitches. The edges of the crochet piece naturally go together side by side and the finished seam will be almost invisible.

project 2: the buttoned cowl

MATERIALS

4 skeins of worsted-weight yarn, 60% alpaca, 40% wool, 80 yd (75m), 1¾ oz (50g), in camel (4)

K-10½ (6.5mm) crochet hook

Yarn needle

1 big, mother-of-pearl button

SIZE

One size

DIMENSIONS

26" circumference x 9½" high (66cm x 24cm)

DIRECTIONS

Work with 2 strands held together.
Make a chain of 25 sts = 9½" (24 cm).
Work in half-double crochet for 47 rows = 26" (66 cm).
Weave in the ends, fold the scarf in half, and sew the 2 ends to make the cowl.
Turn the cowl so the right-side faces out. Sew on a decorative button.

project 3: the scarf

MATERIALS

11 skeins of bulky yarn, 100% wool, 55yd (50m), 1¾ oz (50g), in indigo (5)

1 crochet hook, J-10 (6mm)

Yarn needle

SIZE

One size

DIMENSIONS

9½" x 71" (24cm x 180cm)

DIRECTIONS

Make a chain of 29 sts.
Work the scarf in half-double crochet for 71" (180 cm).

CHAPTER 1

lesson 5

MASTERING THE 6 ESSENTIAL STITCHES

DOUBLE CROCHET

project: make a flat bag*

directions → pages 66–67 • assembly → page 68 • stitch → page 78

MATERIALS

9 skeins of worsted-weight yarn, 60% alpaca, 40% wool, 80 yd (75m), 1¾ oz (50g) in sienna (4)

Size H-8 (5mm) crochet hook

Size K-10½ (6.5mm) crochet hook

Yarn needle

Scissors

Straight pins

STITCH USED

Double crochet

SIZE

One size

GAUGE

9 sts = 4" (10cm) wide

5 rows = 4" (10cm) high

DIMENSIONS

17¾" wide x 19" high (45cm x 48.5cm)

39½" long strap (100cm)

* You will also learn in this lesson how to sew a back stitch. Refer back to this lesson regularly when working on projects.

1/ double crochet (dc)

→ **WORD OF ADVICE!**
Memorize the abbreviation of double crochet, dc, and its symbol.

1 Starting from a foundation chain, yarn over.

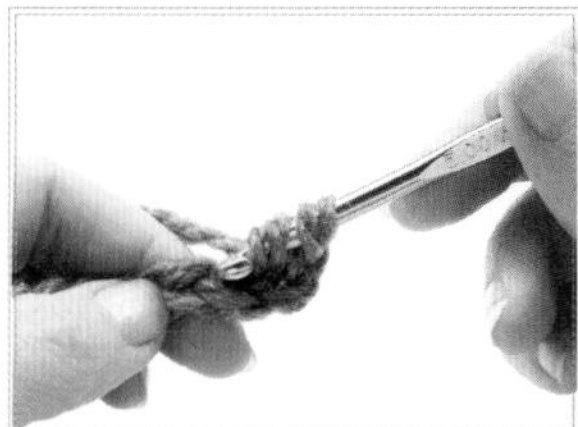

2 Insert the hook into the 4th stitch from the hook.

3 Yarn over again.

4 Pull the yarn through the stitch.

5 There are 3 loops on the hook.

6 Yarn over again.

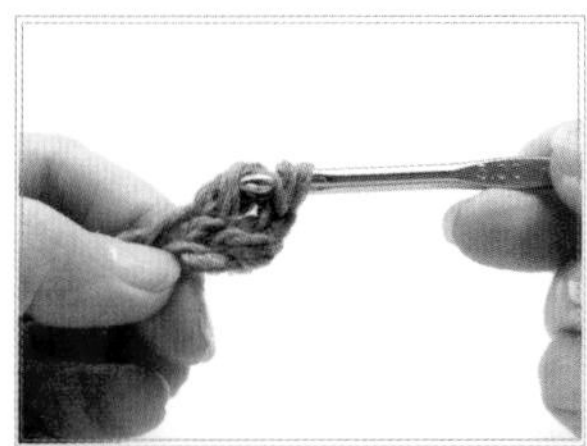

7 Pull the yarn through the first 2 loops.

8 There are 2 loops on the hook.

9 Yarn over again.

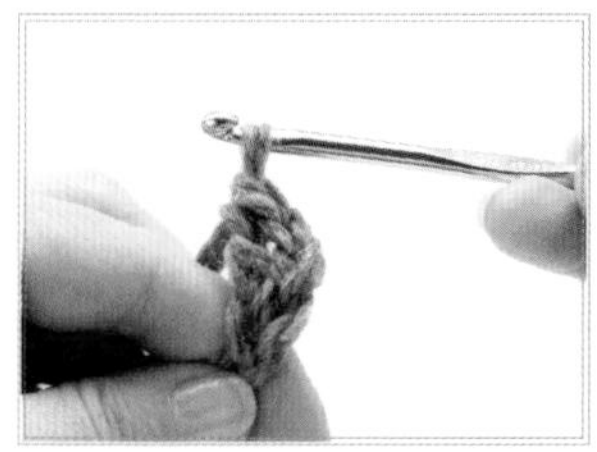

10 Pull the yarn through the 2 loops. There is 1 loop left.

11 Work the last dc in the 3rd ch st from the beginning of the previous row.

12 The dc row is done.

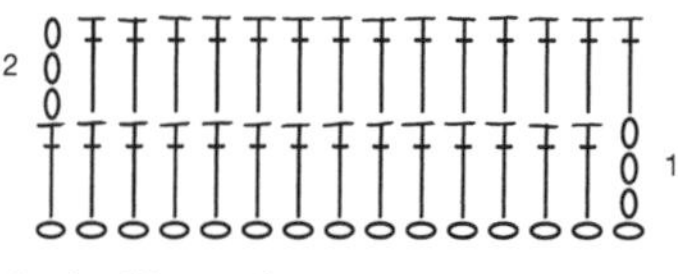

✻ **double crochet**

2/ the flat bag

This bag is composed of 3 parts: the front, the back, and the closure.

Front + half of the shoulder strap
Use 2 strands of yarn held together and the K-10½ (6.5mm) crochet hook.
Make a chain of 40 sts = 17¾" (45cm).
For rows 1–24: Ch 3, work the whole row in dc.
Total length at the end of row 24 = 19" (48.5cm).
For rows 25–50: Continue working on the first 12 sts of the row.
Ch 3 to start, then dc 12 to make the first shoulder strap.
At the end of row 50, the strap will measure 19¾" (50cm) in length.
Stop the piece at the end of row 50.

Back + half of the shoulder strap
Work the second side in the same way as the first.

Closure
Use a single strand and the H-8 (5mm) crochet hook.
Make a chain of 55 sts = 15¾" (40cm) long.
For rows 1–4: Ch 3, work the whole row in dc.
Stop the piece at the end of row 4.

Assemble the sides and the bottom of the bag with backstitch (see instructions at right), as well as the ends of the strap.
Sew the short side of the closure to the center of the back.
Add fringe to the bottom of the bag with leftover yarn strands of different lengths.
Felt the bag (see p. 68).
After felting, the bag will measure 13½" x 15½" (34cm x 39cm).
Sew the closing flap to the back of the bag in the middle of the opening.

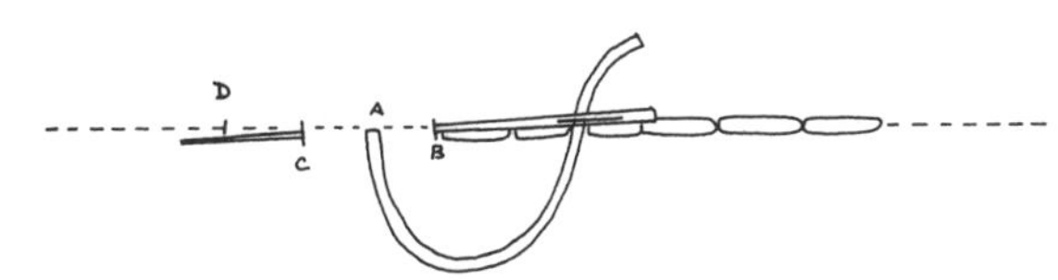

✻ backstitch

1. Pull the needle out at A on the right side of the fabric.
2. Insert into B, to the right of point A, and pull out at C, to the left of point A, at the same distance from A as point B is, so that all the stitches have the same length.
3. Repeat for the desired number of times.

3/ sew the bag

→ **WORD OF ADVICE!**
Before starting to assemble the bag, remember to weave in your ends.

Stack the edges to be sewn, right sides together, and pin in place.
Thread a yarn needle with the same color as the bag.
Slip the yarn into the fabric close to the edge, over 1" (2.5cm), and pull the yarn out on the right side.
Insert the tip of the needle into the 2 pieces and pull the needle out a little bit on the left.
Tighten gently in order to make the first stitch.
Reinsert where the needle came out from the previous stitch. Pull the needle out a little bit away on the left.
Continue as established for the whole length of the sides.
After assembling, turn the work so the right side is facing out.

4/ felting

Wool endures machine washing well, especially with using special settings for delicates and woolens. These settings use cold water, with little to no agitation. In order to felt wool, you must adjust your settings to get exactly what you want for your project.

Felting requires the difference between the hot temperature of the washing and the cold water from rinsing, which shocks the fibers and causes them to shrink. Place the crocheted piece in a protective bag (or a pillowcase that closes for bigger pieces) and then place into the washer. Adjust the machine to the setting reserved for whites at 140° F (60° C). Adjust the level of agitation to the strongest option.

This operation can be carried out while you are doing your next load of towels and sheets if the wool does not run the risk of bleeding dye and discoloring your laundry. Let it dry flat and iron if necessary with a dry cloth placed between the iron and the crocheted piece.

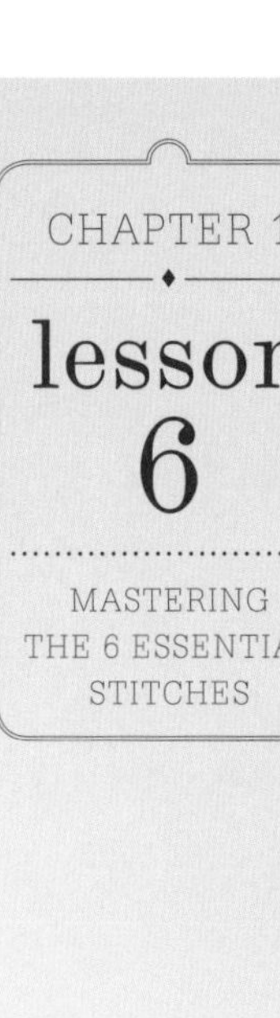

CHAPTER 1

lesson 6

MASTERING THE 6 ESSENTIAL STITCHES

LESSON 6

TREBLE CROCHET

project: make a poncho*

directions → page 72–73 • assembly → page 74 • stitch → page 79

MATERIALS

17 skeins of bulky yarn, 100% wool, 55 yd (50m), 1¾ oz (50g), in plum (5)

Size J-10 (6mm) crochet hook

Yarn needle

Scissors

STITCH USED

Treble crochet

SIZE

One size

GAUGE

10 sts = 4" (10cm) wide

4 rows = 4" (10cm) high

DIMENSIONS

35½" wide x 45½" long (90cm x 114.5cm)

* You will also learn in this lesson how to read an schematic, as well as how to crochet and finish a work with three parts.

1/ treble crochet (tc)

→ **WORD OF ADVICE!**
Memorize the abbreviation of treble crochet, tc, and its symbol.

1 Starting from a foundation chain, yarn over twice.

2 Insert the hook into the 5th stitch from the hook.

3 Yarn over.

4 Pull the yarn through the first stitch.

5 There are 4 loops on the hook. Yarn over again.

6 Pull the yarn through the first 2 loops.

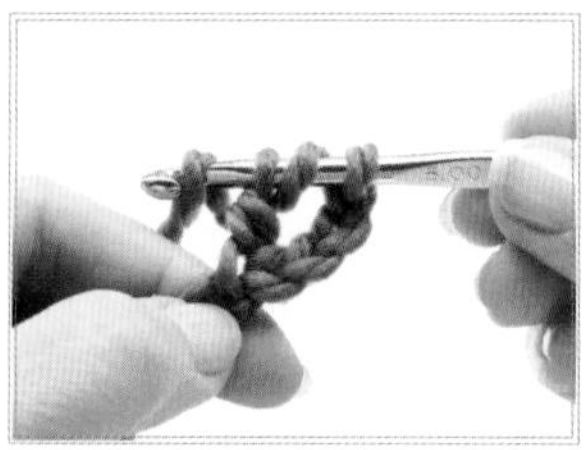

7 There are 3 loops on the hook. Yarn over.

8 Pull the yarn through the first 2 loops.

9 There are 2 loops on the hook.

10 Yarn over again.

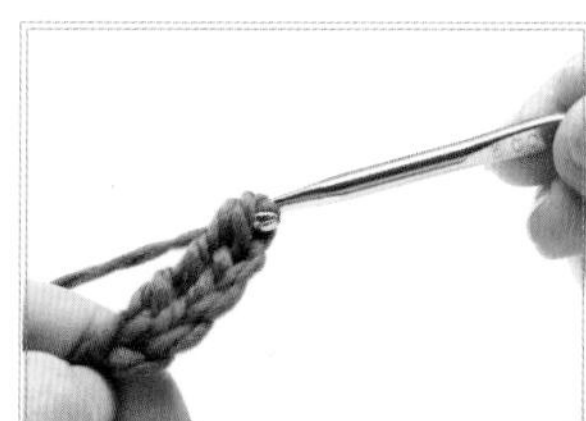

11 Pull the yarn through the 2 loops.

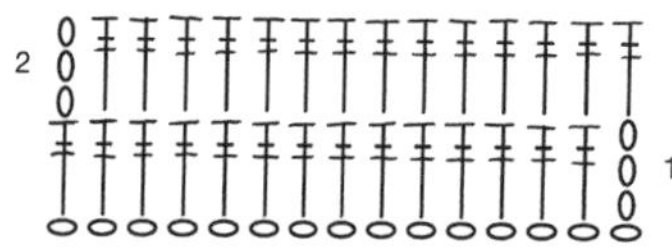

✻ **treble crochet**

12 There is 1 loop on the hook.

13 Continue as such until the end of the row.

14 In order to finish the row, yarn over twice.

15 Insert into the last ch st from the beginning of the previous row in order to make the last tc.

16 End after the tc. In order to start the following row, you must ch 4.

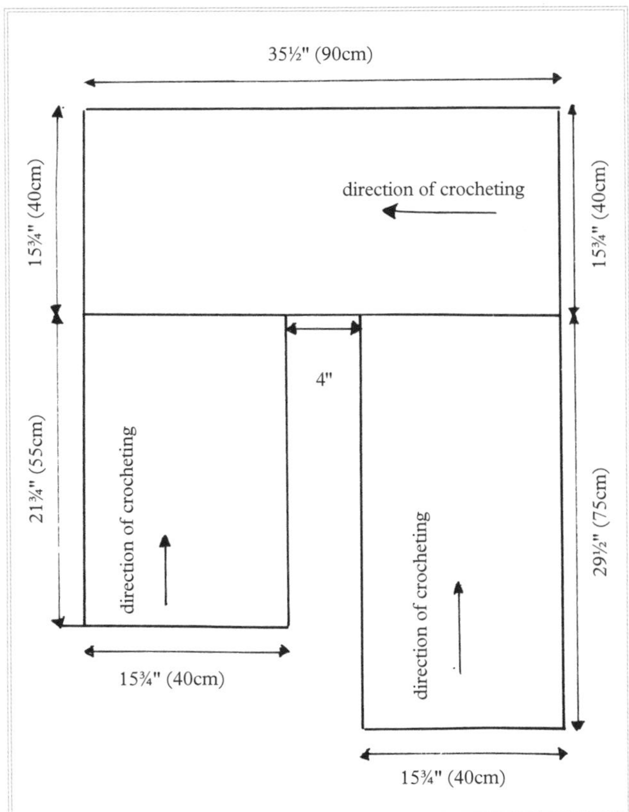

* schematic for assembly

2/ the poncho

The poncho is formed from 3 rectangles of the same width but different lengths.

Front left
Make a chain of 41 sts = 15¾" (40cm) wide.
For rows 1–23: Ch 4, work the entire row in tc. Stop the work at the end of row 23.
This side will measure 21¾" (55cm) long.

Right front
Make a chain of 41 sts = 15¾" (40cm) wide.
For rows 1–30: Ch 4, work the entire row in tc. Stop the work at the end of row 30.
This side will measure 29½" (75cm) long.

Back
Make a chain of 41 sts = 15¾" (40cm) wide.
For rows 1–35: Ch 4, work the entire row in tc. Stop the work at the end of row 35. The back will measure 35½" (90cm) long.

3/ assemble and graft

Place the width of each front side against one of the lengths of the back, leaving the 3 center rows (4" [10cm]) free in order to make the neck. Assemble the pieces by grafting (p. 59).

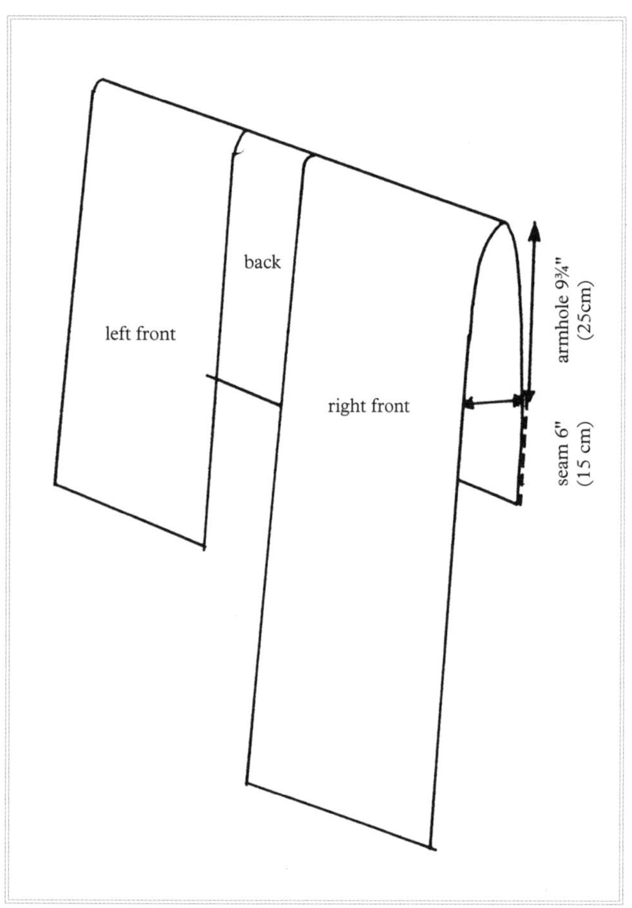

✻ **schematic for assembly**

In order to have a poncho that can be worn like a cardigan, create armholes by seaming the back and front sides for 6" (15cm) up from the bottom of the back.

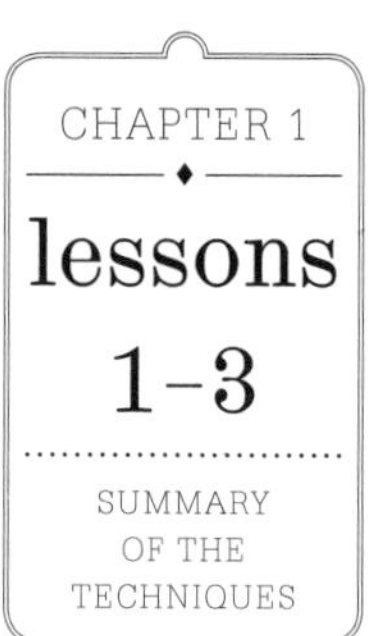

→ WORD OF ADVICE!
Here are the 6 basic crochet stitches.
When you know how to execute them perfectly, you will be able to make virtually anything. All crochet is simply a combination of these different stitches.

1/ chain stitch (ch) ○

Make a slip knot with the hook and keep the hook in the resulting loop (1). Yarn over by passing the head of the crochet hook under the strand attached to the ball and pull the crochet hook in order to pull the yarn through the loop. The first ch st is formed (2). Continue as such to make as many ch sts as indicated in the directions (3).

1.

2.

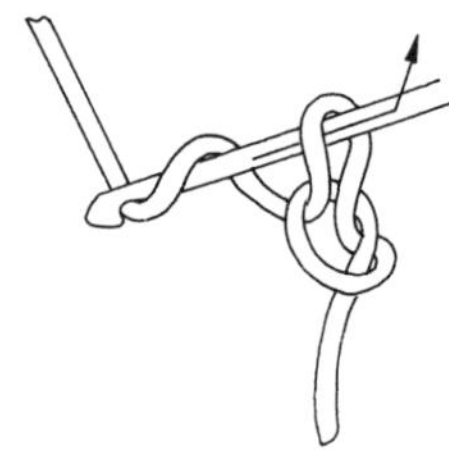

3.

2/ slip stitch (sl st) ●

Starting from a foundation chain, insert the hook into the 2nd ch st (1), and yarn over. Pull the yarn simultaneously through the ch st and the loop that is on the hook (2). There is only one loop on the hook (3). Repeat the previous step in order to make the next sl st. End the row by inserting the hook into the last ch st, yarn over and pull it through the ch st and the loop that is on the hook.

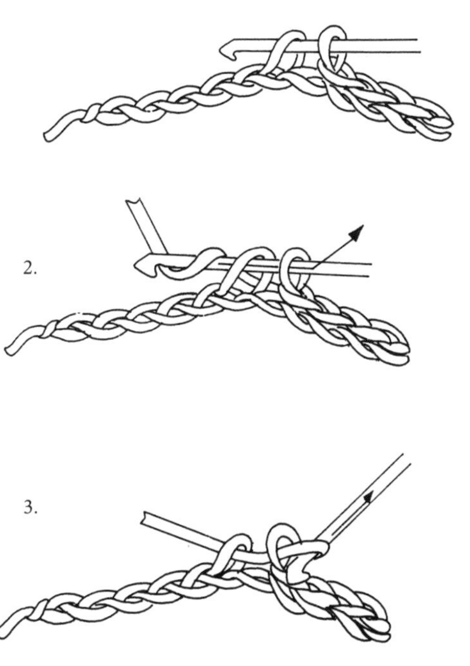

3/ single crochet (sc) X or +

Starting from a foundation chain, insert the hook into the 2nd ch st from the hook. Yarn over, and pull the yarn through the ch st (1). There are 2 loops on the hook. Yarn over, pull the yarn through the 2 loops (2). There is 1 loop on the hook. Insert into the next stitch and proceed in the same manner until the end of the row by working the whole row in sc. At the end of the row, insert in the last ch st and do sc 1. Ch 1, then turn the work in order to proceed from right to left.

1.

2.

4/ half-double crochet (hdc) ⊤

Starting from a foundation chain, yarn over, insert the hook into the 3rd ch st from the hook, yarn over again, and pull the yarn through the stitch (1). There are 3 loops on the hook. Yarn over again and pull the yarn through the 3 loops (2). There is 1 loop on the hook. For the following hdc, yarn over, insert into the next stitch, and proceed as for the first stitch (3). Finish the row by working the last hdc in the ch st from the beginning of the previous row. Ch 2 then turn the work in order to start a new row.

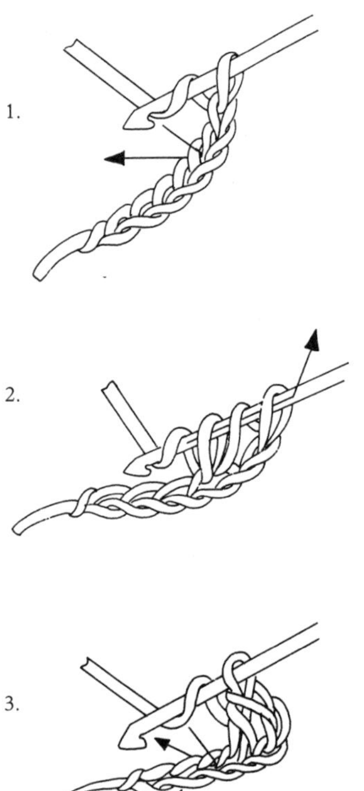

5/ double crochet (dc) ⫫

Starting from a foundation chain, yarn over, insert the hook into the 4th ch st from the hook (1), yarn over again, and pull the yarn through the stitch. There are 3 loops on the hook (2). Yarn over again and pull the yarn through the first 2 loops (3). There are 2 loops on the hook. Yarn over again and pull the yarn through the remaining 2 loops (4). There is 1 loop on the hook (5). For the following dc, yarn over, insert into the next stitch and proceed as for the first stitch.
Finish the row by working the last dc in the last ch st from the beginning of the previous row. Ch 3, turn the work in order to start the new row.

1.

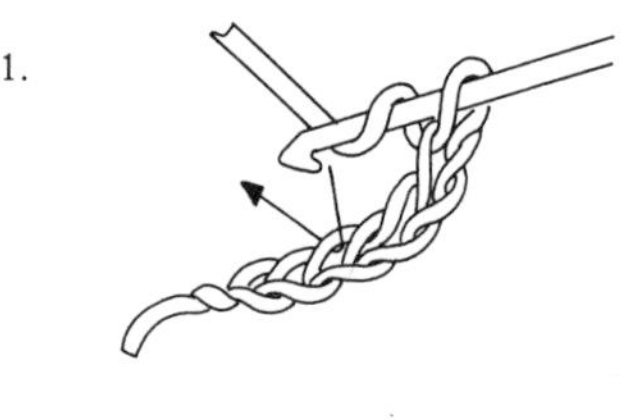

2.

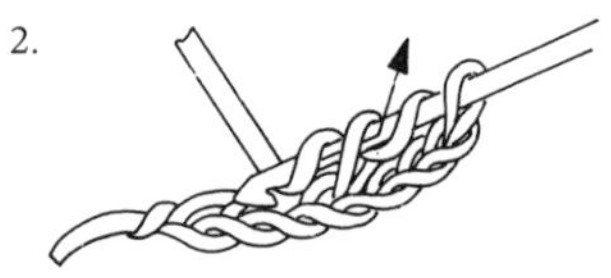

3.

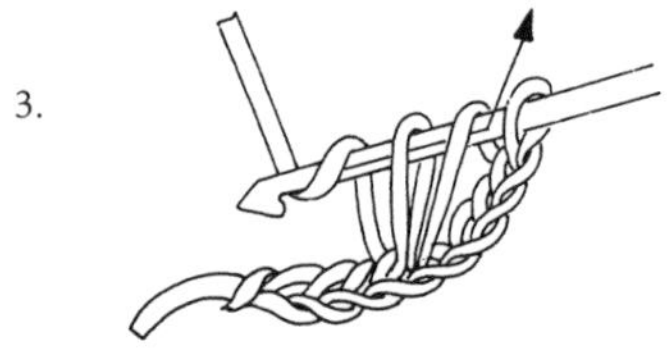

4.

6/ treble crochet (tc)

Starting from a foundation chain, yarn over twice, insert the hook into the 5th ch st from the hook (1), yarn over again, and pull the yarn through the stitch. There are 4 loops on the hook. Yarn over again and pull the yarn through the first 2 loops (2). There are 3 loops on the hook. Yarn over again and pull the yarn through the following 2 loops (3). There are 2 loops on the hook. Yarn over again and pass it through the last 2 loops (4). There is 1 loop on the hook (5). For the next tc, work as for the first stitch.
Finish the row by working the last tc in the last ch st from the beginning of the previous row. Ch 4, turn the work in order to start the new row.

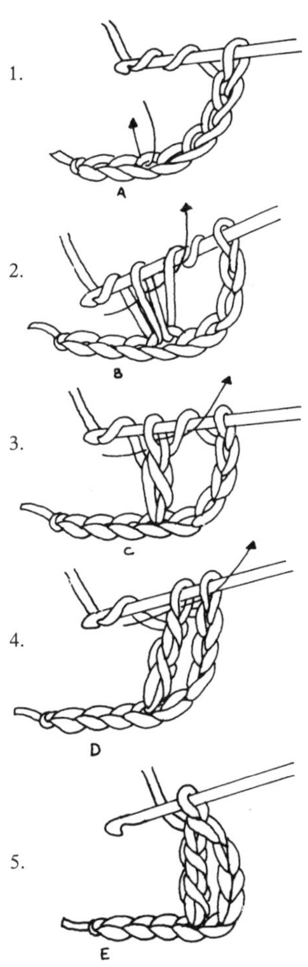

CHAPTER 2

DECREASES AND INCREASES

CHAPTER 2
lesson
7
DECREASES
AND INCREASES

HORIZONTAL RIBBING

project: make a marled tote bag*

directions → pages 84–85 • assembly → page 87 • schematic → page 87

MATERIALS

4 skeins of fingering weight yarn, 55% viscose, 45% cotton, 170 yd (156m), 1¾ oz (50g), 2 skeins each in dark brown and lavender

5 skeins of bulky yarn, 30% yak down, 70% wool, 70 yd (63m), 1¾ oz (50g), in earthy brown

3 skeins of worsted weight bouclé yarn, 80% wool, 20% camel down, 110 yd (100m), 1¾ (50g), in plum

Size N-13 (10mm) crochet hook

Yarn needle

1 pair of leather handles, ¾" wide x 15½" long (39.5cm x 2cm), with metal loops

Scissors

Straight pins

STITCHES USED

Single crochet

Horizontal ribbing

Back loop single crochet

SIZE

One size

GAUGE

7 sts = 4" (10cm) wide

8 rows = 4" (10cm) high

DIMENSIONS

12" wide x 19" long x 4¾" deep (30.5cm x 49.5cm x 12cm)

* In this lesson you will also learn how to make your own marled yarn.

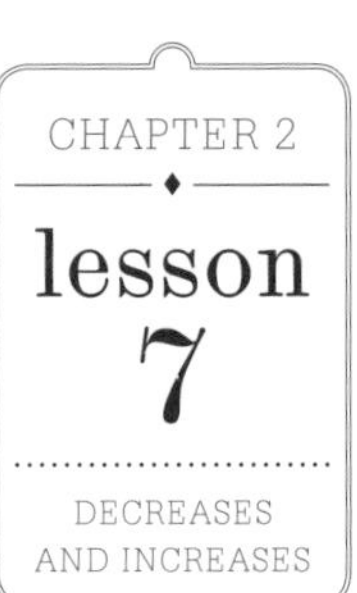

1/ start the tote bag

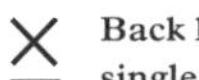
Back loop single crochet

→ **WORD OF ADVICE!**
Work simultaneously with all strands of the 4 colors with the size N-13 (10mm) hook.

1 Make a chain of 39 sts = 19¾" (50cm). For row 1, ch 1 then sc in every stitch.

2 Ch 1 to turn and start row 2.

3 Work the whole row in sc using the back loop of each stitch: Insert the hook under the back part of the stitch from the previous row.

4 Yarn over.

5 Pull the yarn through the first stitch. There are 2 loops on the hook.

6 Yarn over, pull the yarn through the 2 loops.

7 There is 1 loop on the hook.

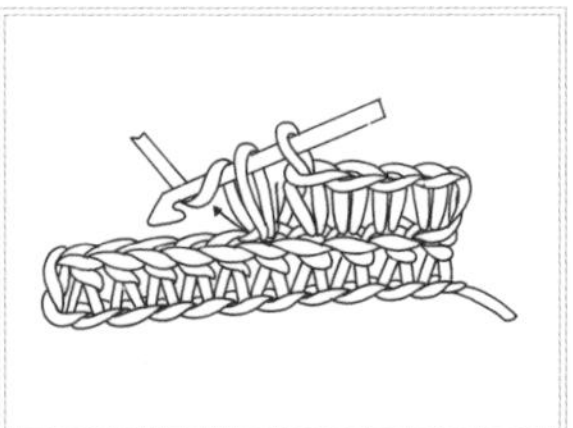

8 Insert into the back loop of the next stitch and do the same thing with this second stitch as well as with all the following ones.

9 At the end of the row, insert into the last stitch (that is, the ch st from the beginning of the previous row), and sc 1 by inserting normally.

10 Ch 1, then turn the work in order to proceed from right to left. Continue to work in horizontal ribbing by following steps 3–10. Repeat until 24 rows have been worked.

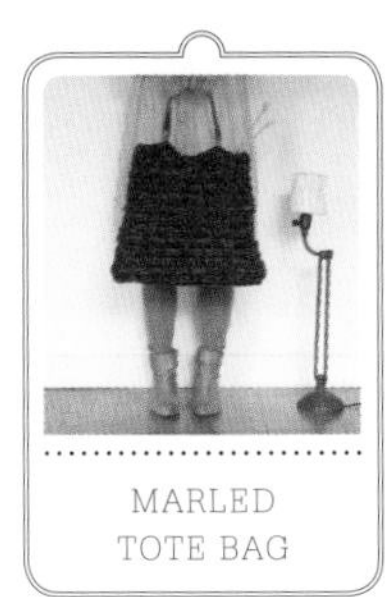
MARLED
TOTE BAG

2/ make a decrease

→ **WORD OF ADVICE!**
Decreases take away one or several stitches in a row in order to reduce the width of the piece.

1 On row 25, ch 1, work the next 33 sts in horizontal ribbing. Do not work over the last 6 sts of the row in order to make a decrease.

2 Ch 1 to turn and start row 26.

3 Work the next 27 sts in horizontal ribbing; do not work over the last 6 sts of the row in order to make a decrease. Ch 1 to turn.

3/ make an increase

→ **WORD OF ADVICE!**
Increases add one or several stitches on a row in order to add width to the place.

1 For row 27, work the whole row in horizontal ribbing. At the end of the row, ch 6 in order to increase.

2 Ch 1 more to turn.

3 Start row 28 with sc 6 over the next 6 ch sts then work the following 27 sts in horizontal ribbing. At the end of the row, ch 6 and ch 1 more to turn. For row 29, sc 6 over the next 6 ch sts then work the following 33 sts in horizontal ribbing. For rows 30–54, ch 1 and work the 39 sts of the row in horizontal ribbing. Break the yarn at the end of row 54.

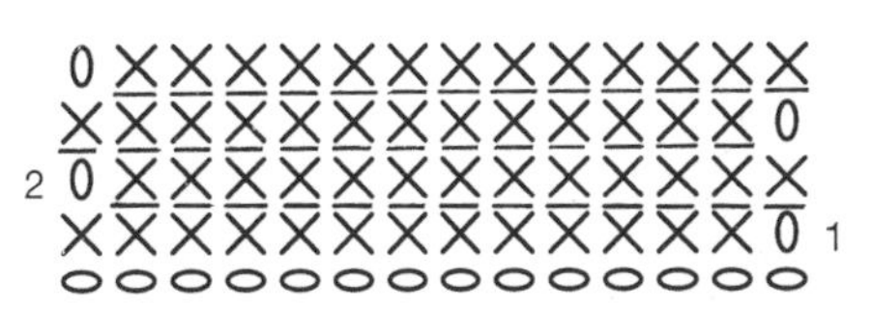

*** back loop single crochet/horizontal ribbing**

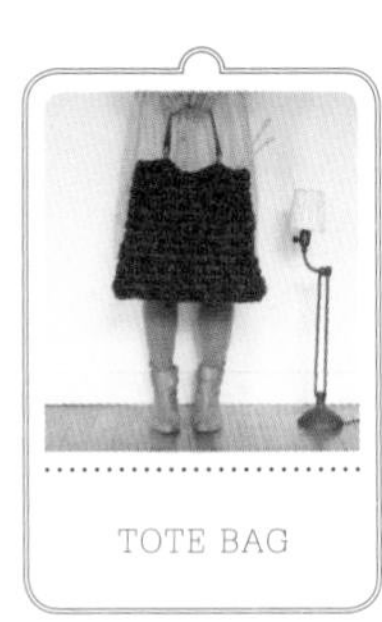

4/ sew the tote bag

→ **WORD OF ADVICE!**
Before starting to seam your tote bag, weave in the ends.

Place the back and the front of the bag on top of each other, right sides together, and pin the sides together. Next, pin the bottom of the bag to the bottom of the sides in order to give depth to the bag (below, far right). Thread a yarn needle with two strands of sportweight yarn, then assemble with a back stitch (p. 68). When seaming is complete, turn the bag right side out.

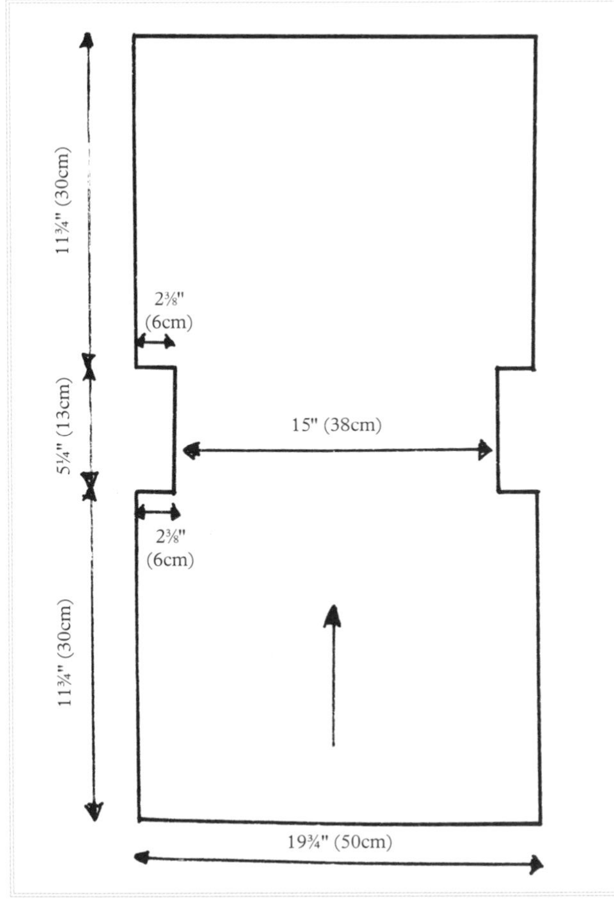

5/ attach the handles

1 Place a pin as a reference mark 4" (10cm) from one of the ends of the tote bag.

2 Slide a loop of the handle under the stitches on the right side, ¾" (2cm) from the top edge of the bag.

3 In order to affix the loop to the wrong side, make several stitches with a yarn needle working around the whole ring.

4 Finish with the yarn needle by making 2 fastening stitches. Sew the other loop of the handle in the same way, then the second handle on the opposite side of the tote bag.

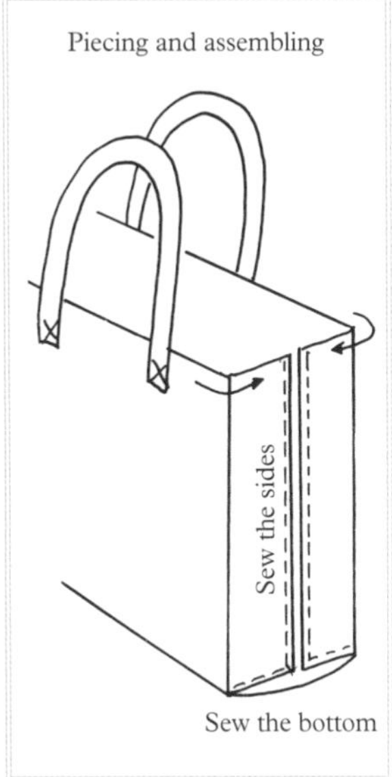

CHAPTER 2

lesson 8

DECREASES AND INCREASES

LESSON 8

VERTICAL RIBBING

project: make a pair of legwarmers*

directions → pages 90–91 • assembly → page 91

MATERIALS

9 skeins of bulky yarn, 100% wool, 55 yd (50m), 1¾ oz (50g) in plum (5)

Size J-10 (6mm) crochet hook

Yarn needle

Scissors

Straight pins

STITCHES USED

Single crochet

Vertical ribbing

SIZE

One size

GAUGE

11 sts = 4" (10cm) wide

12 rows = 4" (10cm) high

DIMENSIONS

17¾" high x 13" circumference (45cm x 15cm)

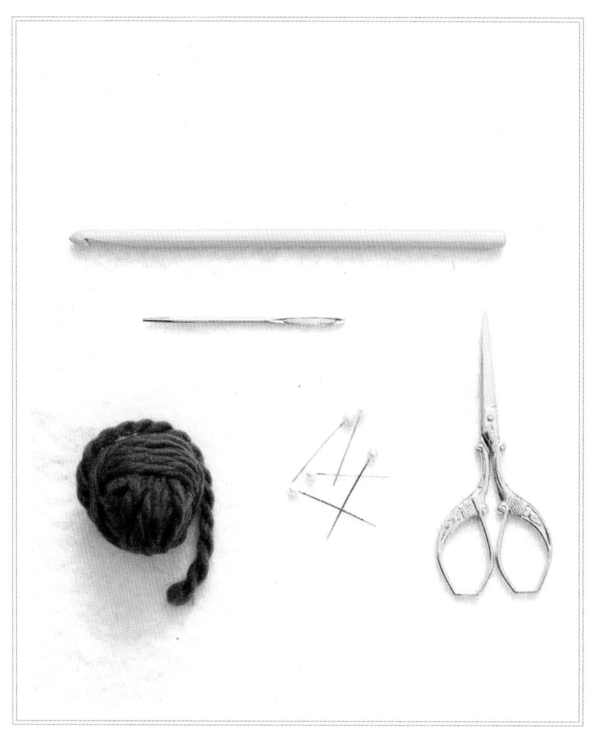

* You will learn another way of making textured stitches.

1/ legwarmers

Front Post Double Crochet (fpdc)

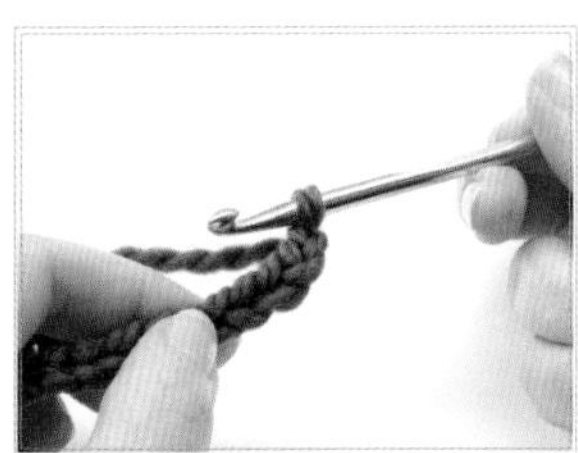

1 Make a chain of 36 sts = 13" (33cm). For row 1, insert into the 2nd ch st from the hook and sc 1. Continue with sc for the whole row, ending with 1 sc in the last ch st.

2 Ch 1 to turn, and work all of row 2 in sc. End by working the last sc in the ch st from the beginning of row 1.

3 For row 3, ch 1 to turn.

4 Sc 1 in the next stitch.

5 Start with 1 fpdc in the next stitch with a yarn over.

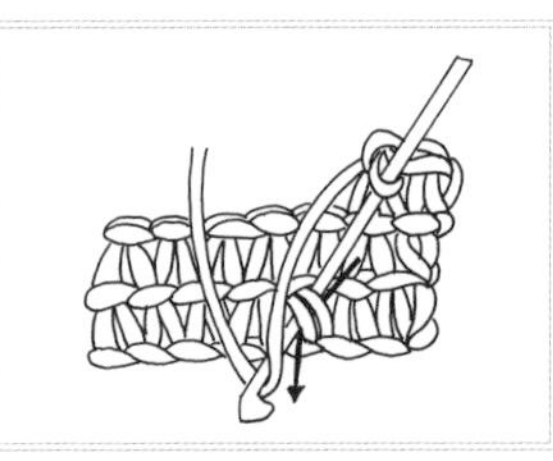

6 Slide the hook from right to left behind the vertical post of the sc from row 1.

7 Yarn over again.

8 Pull the yarn through the sc.

9 There are 3 loops on the hook. Yarn over and pull the yarn through the first 2 loops. There are 2 loops on the hook. Yarn over again and pull the yarn through the remaining 2 loops.

10 There is 1 loop on the hook.

11 Sc 1 in the next 2 stitches. Repeat from step 5 across the whole row ending the row with a sc. Ch 1 to turn and work row 4 in sc.

12 For row 5, ch 1 to turn, sc 1 in the next stitch, then fpdc: yarn over and slide the hook from right to left behind the vertical post of the fpdc from row 3.

13 For the following rows, repeat rows 4 and 5.
Work 57 rows of vertical ribbing for one legwarmer = 17¾" x 13" (45cm x 33cm).
Make a second, identical legwarmer.

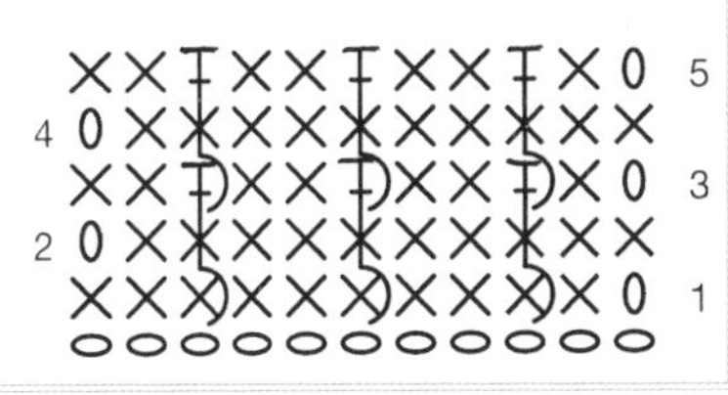

⁕ **front post double crochet**

2/ sewing the legwarmers

→ **WORD OF ADVICE!**
Before starting to assemble, carefully weave in the ends.

1 Fold the rectangles in half lengthwise, right sides together, so that there are 2 strips of 6½" x 17¾" (16.5cm x 45cm).

2 Sew with a back stitch (p. 68).

3 Turn the legwarmers right side out.

CHAPTER 2

lesson 9

DECREASES AND INCREASES

LESSON 9

CHEVRONS

project 1: make a simple hat*

directions → pages 94–95 • assembly → pages 95–97 • variations → pages 98, 100, 102

MATERIALS

2 skeins of fingering yarn, 100% merino wool, 90 yd (82m), 1¾ oz (50g), in light brown and purple (2)

2 skeins of fingering yarn, 100% merino wool, 90 yd (82m), 1¾ oz (50g), in charcoal (2)

Size E-4 (3.5mm) crochet hook

Yarn needle

2 cardboard rings for the pompoms, outside diameter of 4¾" (12cm)

Scissors

Straight pins

STITCH USED

Chevron stitch

SIZE

One size

GAUGE

21 sts = 4" (10cm) wide

9 rows = 4" (10 cm) high

DIMENSIONS

9½" high x 22½" around (24cm x 56cm)

* You will discover, thanks to this lesson, that with some little changes in the size and color palette, you can have 4 different versions of the same project!

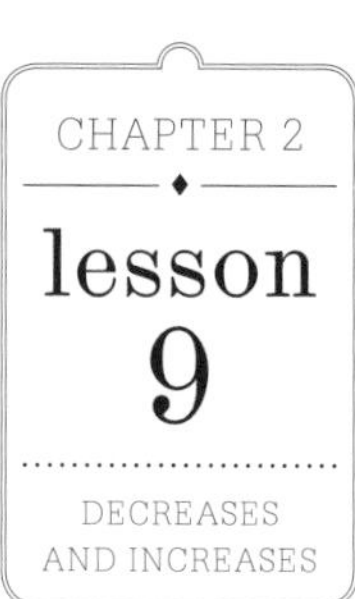

1/ the hat

→ **WORD OF ADVICE!**
On the 2nd row, the waves from the chevrons will begin to appear.

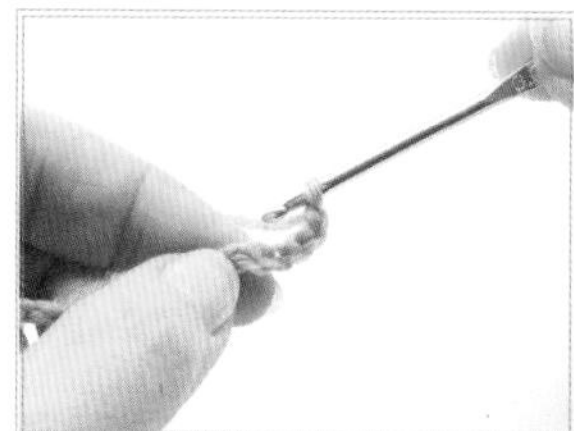

1 Make a chain of 101 sts (multiple of 10 sts + 1 st) in light brown.

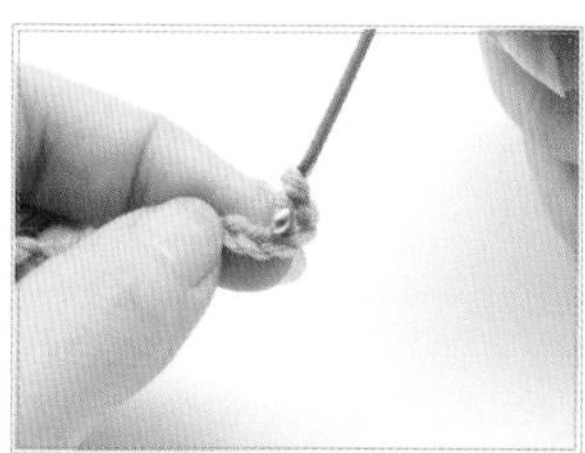

2 For row 1, yarn over, insert the hook into the 4th ch st from the hook.

3 Dc 1, then dc 1 in the next 3 sts.

4 Start to work 3 dc together by starting with a yarn over.

5 Insert the hook into the next stitch.

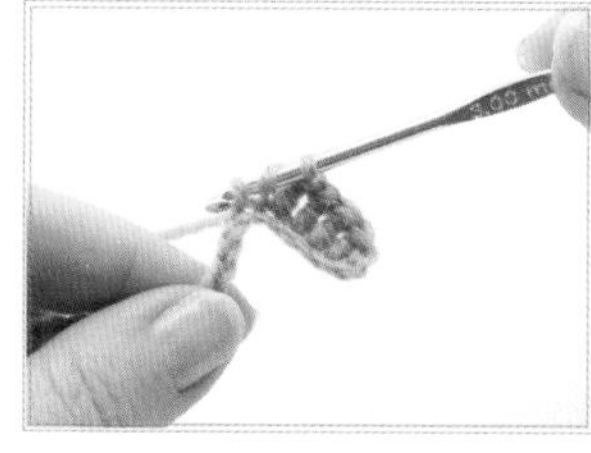

6 Yarn over and pull the yarn through the stitch.

7 Yarn over, pull the yarn through the first 2 loops.

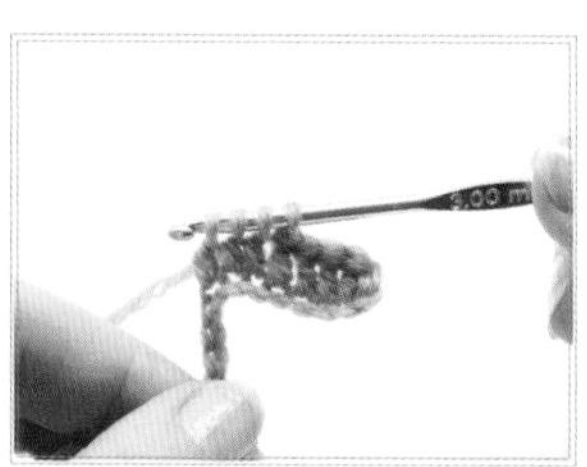

8 Redo steps 5–7 two more times in the next 2 stitches. There are 4 loops.

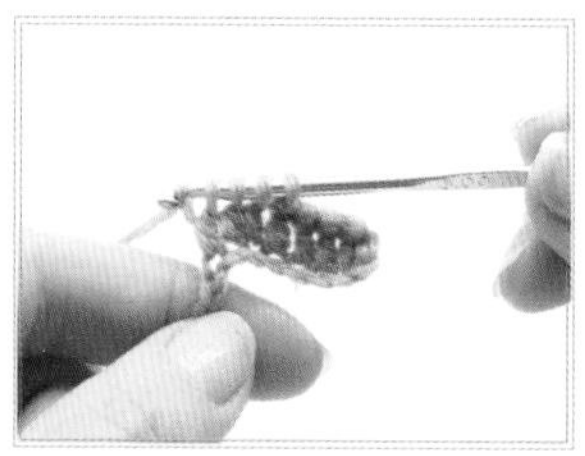

9 Yarn over.

10 Pull the yarn through the 4 loops from the hook. There is 1 loop. You just worked 3 dc together (dc3tog).

11 Continue working into the base chain. Dc 1 in each one of the next 3 sts.

12 Make a shell in the next stitch by working 3 dc into the same stitch.

13 Continue working into the base chain. Dc 1 in each of the next 3 stitches. Repeat steps 4–13.

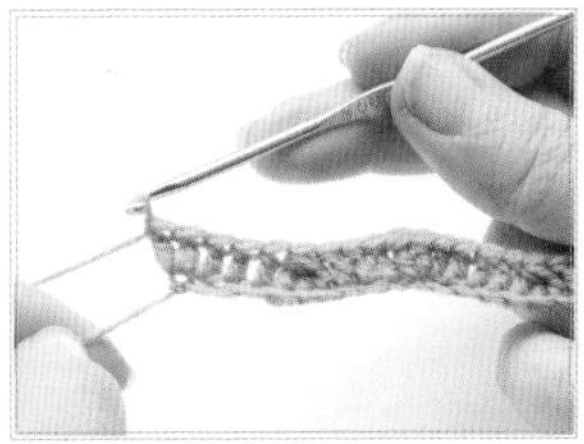

14 Finish the row by working 2 dc into the last ch st.

15 For row 2, ch 3 to turn.

16 Dc 1 into the first st.

17 Dc 1 in each 1 of the next 3 stitches, then dc3tog.

18 Dc 1 in each 1 of the next 3 stitches, 1 shell of 3 dc in the next stitch, dc 1 in the next 3 stitches.

19 Repeat steps 17–18 across the whole row ending with 2 dc into the 2nd ch st from the beginning of row 1. Repeat row 2 changing yarn on row 3 to purple. On row 5, change yarn to charcoal and continue. Work 24 rows in total, then cut the yarn. Rectangle will measure 9½" x 22" (24cm x 56cm).

2/ sew the hat

Weave in the ends. Fold the rectangle in half. To assemble, sew the side by grafting with 1 strand of charcoal (p. 59). Leave the top of the cap open.

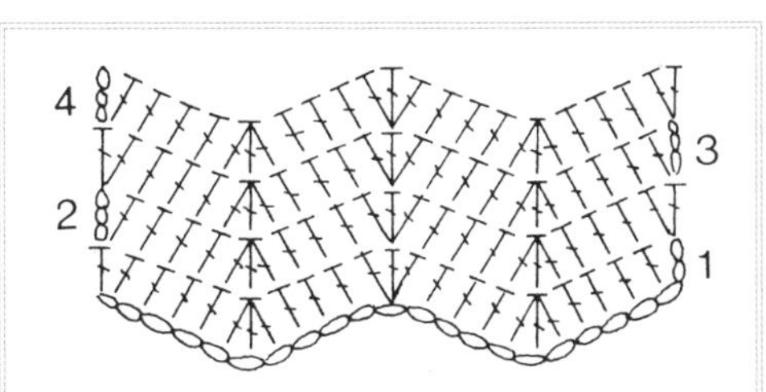

* **chevron stitch**

3/ make a cord

Cut a section of purple yarn 6½ yd (6m) long.
Fold it into fourths, and attach one of the ends to a fixed point.
Hold onto the strands and twist them counter-clockwise.
Then the surface of the yarn will begin to kink back on itself. Fold the cord in half. Let go of the ends. The cord will twist upon itself.
Detach the cord from its support, make a knot at each end, and cut the ends to even out the strands.

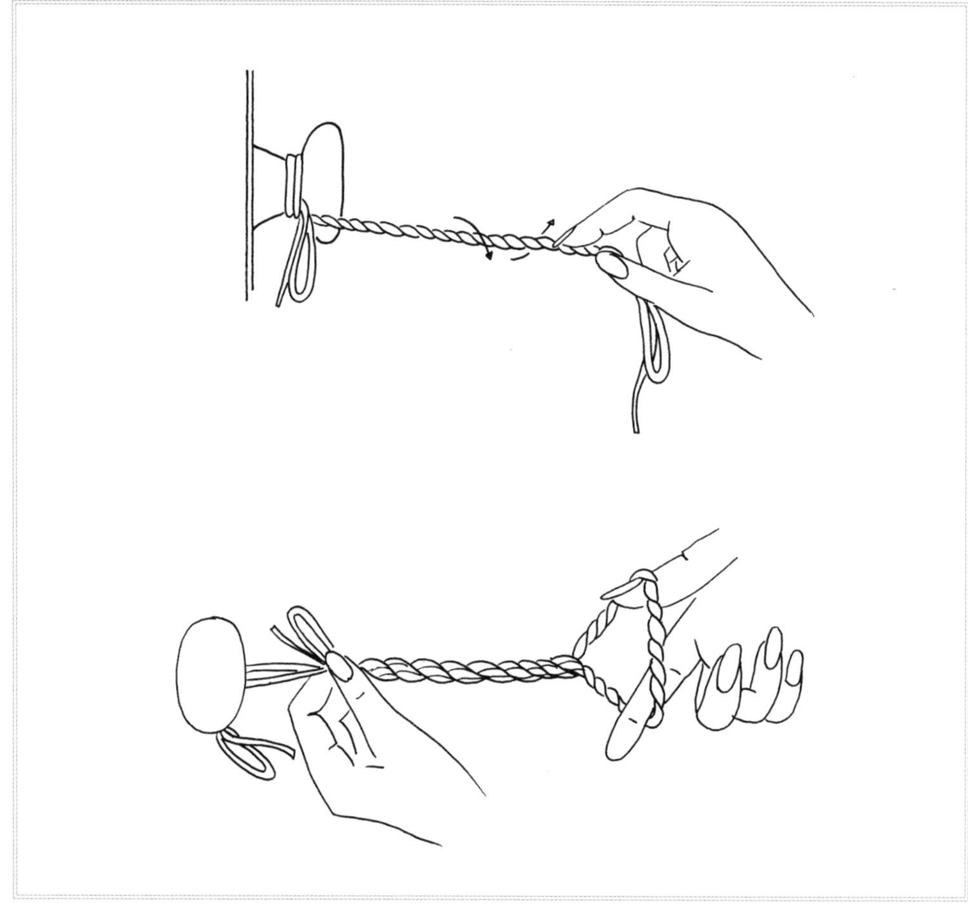

4/ make the pom-poms

Place two cardboard rings one against the other, and wrap the two rings with charcoal and purple until they are entirely covered (1). Slide the tip of a pair of scissors between the two pieces of cardboard and, holding the center of the pom-pom closed with the other hand, cut the yarn all the way around (2). Fold strand of dark brown yarn in half, slide it between the 2 circles, and tie it very tightly (3). Even out the strands of yarn in the pom-pom (4). Make a second pom-pom in the same way. With the help of a yarn needle, weave the cord around the top of the cap, 2¼" (5.5cm) from the top edge, and tie it to close the cap. To finish, sew a pom-pom to each end of the cord.

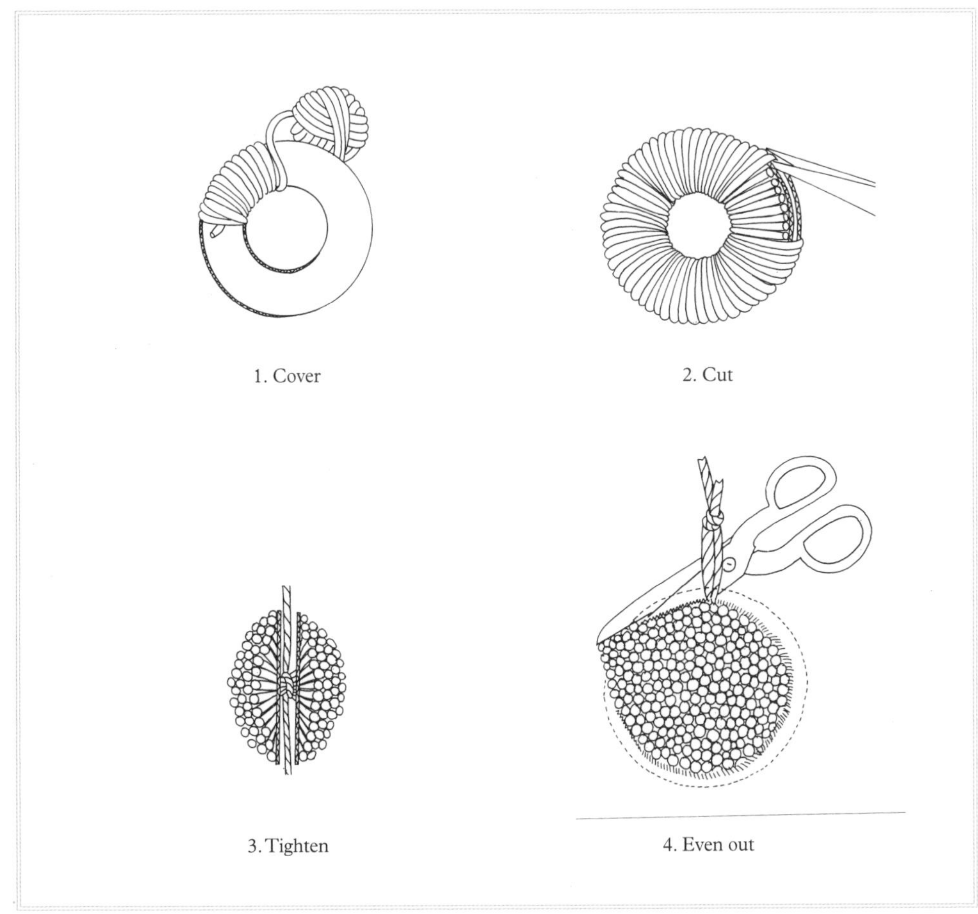

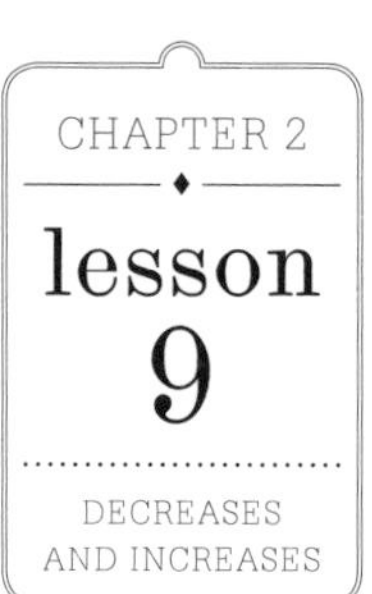

project 2: 3-color hat

MATERIALS

1 skein of sportweight yarn, 100% merino wool, 90 yd (82m), 1¾ oz (50g), in purple, light brown, and charcoal

Size E-4 (3.5mm) crochet hook

Yarn needle

2 buttons, 2" (5cm) in diameter

Straight pins

SIZE

One size

DIMENSIONS

9½" high x 22" circumference (24cm x 56cm)

DIRECTIONS

Make a chain of 101 sts in charcoal. Work in chevron stitch, regularly changing colors as follows: 2 rows charcoal, 2 rows light brown, and 2 rows purple. Repeat these stripes 4 times total = 9½" (24cm) in height total. Fold the strip in two and seam the edge by grafting. Close the hat by sewing a decorative button 2" (5cm) from the top on the front and the back.

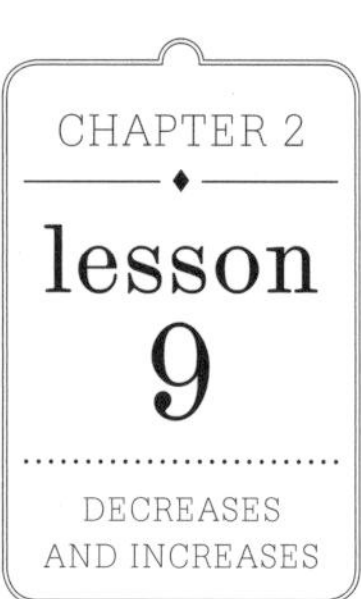

project 3: trapper hat

MATERIALS

3 balls sportweight yarn, 100% merino wool, 90 yd (82m), 1¾ oz (50g), in light brown (2)

Size E-4 (3.5mm) crochet hook

Yarn needle

2 buttons, ½"–¾" in diameter (13mm–2cm)

Straight pins

SIZE

One size

DIMENSIONS

9½" high x 22" circumference (24 x 56cm)

DIRECTIONS

Make a chain of 101 sts in light brown and work in chevron stitch as for the 3-color hat (p. 98). Once the body of the cap is finished, add the flaps: skip 15 sts, and work the first flap in chevron stitch for 21 sts and for 21 rows. Fasten off.

To make the other flap, skip 29 sts and work chevron stitch over 21 sts and for 21 rows. Skip the last 15 sts. Fold the strip in half and seam the edge by grafting.

Sew the 2 buttons to the bottom of a flap. Slipping the buttons from the other flap between two dc from the chevrons will be sufficient instead of making buttonholes.

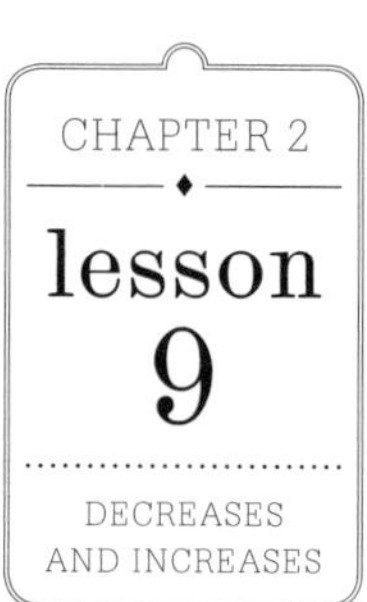

project 4: the long hat

MATERIALS

8 skeins of fingering yarn, 100% merino wool, 90 yd (82m), 1¾ oz (50g), 6 skeins in charcoal and 1 skein each in purple and light brown (2)

Size E-4 (3.5mm) crochet hook

Yarn needle

Straight pins

SIZE

One size

DIMENSIONS

27½" long x 22" circumference (70cm x 56cm)

DIRECTIONS

Make a chain of 101 sts in light brown. Work in chevron stitch: 2 rows light brown, 2 rows purple, and continue in charcoal. When hat reaches 26" (66cm) in length, work 2 rows in purple and finish the work with 2 rows in light brown.

Fold the strip in two and seam the side by grafting. Make cord with charcoal and tie it around the bottom of the cap in order to close it.

CHAPTER 2

lesson 10

DECREASES AND INCREASES

LESSON 10

FLORET STITCH

project: make a pair of mittens

directions → page 106–109 • schematics → page 107–108 • assembly → page 109

MATERIALS

4 skeins of bulky yarn, 100% wool, 55 yd (50m), 1¾ oz (50g), in light blue (5)

Size J-10 (6mm) crochet hook

Yarn needle

Scissors

Straight pins

STITCHES USED

Single crochet

Double crochet

Floret stitch

SIZE

One size

GAUGE

11 stitches = 4" (10cm) wide

8 rows = 4" (10cm) high

DIMENSIONS

10½" circumference (26.5cm)

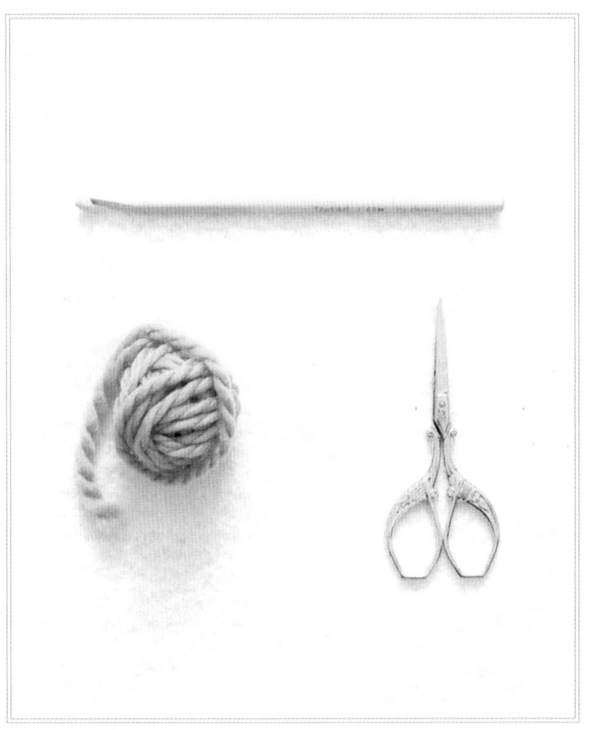

1/ make the right mitten with florets

1 Make a chain of 29 sts. Work 5 rows in sc.

2 On row 6, start the floret stitch: work 1 row in dc.

3 On row 7, ch 1 to turn.

4 Skip 1 stitch, dc 1 in the next stitch, then sl st in the next stitch.

5 Repeat step 4 six times more (without skipping a stitch) and end the row with sc 14.

6 Works rows 8 and 9 as for rows 6 and 7 (steps 2–5). Work row 10 as for row 6 (step 2). For row 11, ch 1 to turn, skip 1 st, then *dc 1 in the next stitch, sl st into the next stitch*. Repeat from * to * 7 times total.

7 Make the thumb opening as follows: ch 4.

8 Skip 4 sts.

9 Sc 1 in the next stitch then end the row with sc 10.

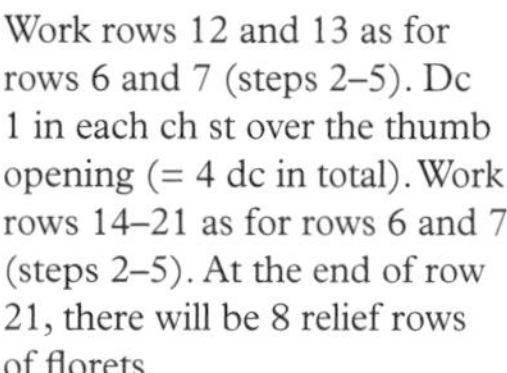

Work rows 12 and 13 as for rows 6 and 7 (steps 2–5). Dc 1 in each ch st over the thumb opening (= 4 dc in total). Work rows 14–21 as for rows 6 and 7 (steps 2–5). At the end of row 21, there will be 8 relief rows of florets.

10 On row 22, work only on the first 14 stitches of the row to make the tip of the mitten. Start the decreases. Ch 2 to turn.

MITTENS

11 Dc 1 in the next stitch.

12 In order to work the next 2 dc together, first yarn over.

13 Insert the hook into the next stitch.

14 Pull through a loop.

15 There are 3 loops on the hook. Yarn over.

16 Pull the yarn through the first 2 loops, there are 2 loops on the hook.

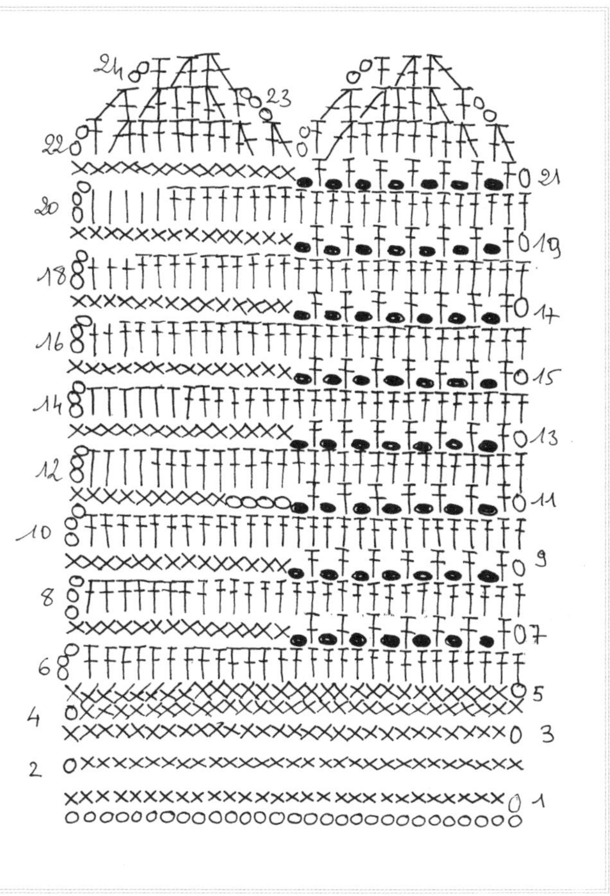

* schematic for the right mitten

7.

4/

17 Continue by repeating steps 12 to 15 one more time by starting in the next stitch. There are 3 loops on the hook.

18 Yarn over and pull the yarn through the 3 loops on the hook. There is 1 loop on the hook.

19 Continue working across the row by dc 1 in the next 6 stitches then dc2tog twice. The point of the mitten is taking shape.
For row 23, ch 3 to turn, dc 1 in the next stitch, dc2tog, dc in the next 2 stitches, then dc2tog twice.
For row 24, ch 1, dc in the next stitch, dc2tog twice. At the end of the row, break the yarn.
Join the yarn on row 22 to the 14 stitches that have not been worked. Work in the same way row 22 to row 24 in order to make the other half of the mitten top.

2/ make the left mitten

Work the left mitten in the same way as the right mitten, but with the 14 stitches of the florets at the end of the row instead of at the beginning in order to make a mirror image.

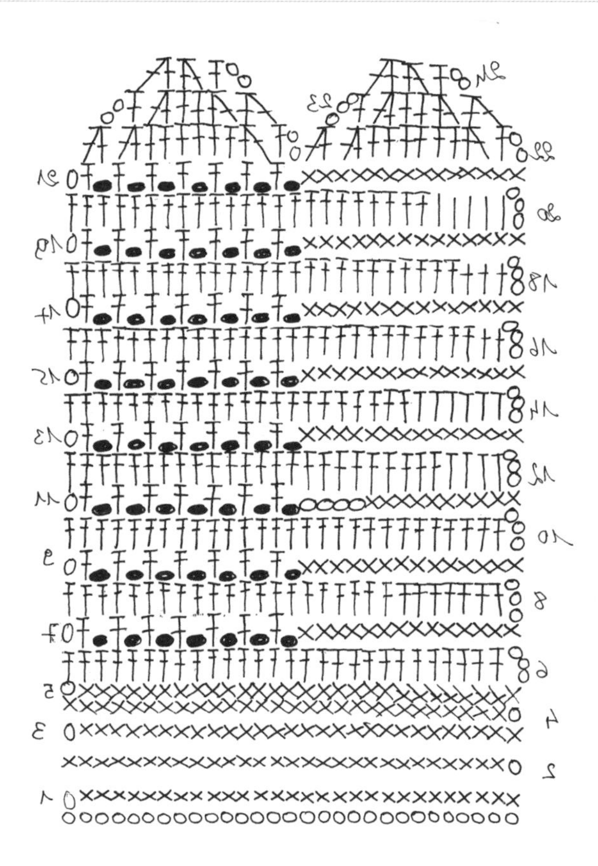

✻ **schematic for the left mitten**

MITTENS

3/ the thumbs

→ **WORD OF ADVICE!**
The thumbs are made separately and will be sewn onto the mittens.

1 Make a chain of 9 sts. Secure the last stitch to the first with 1 sl st.

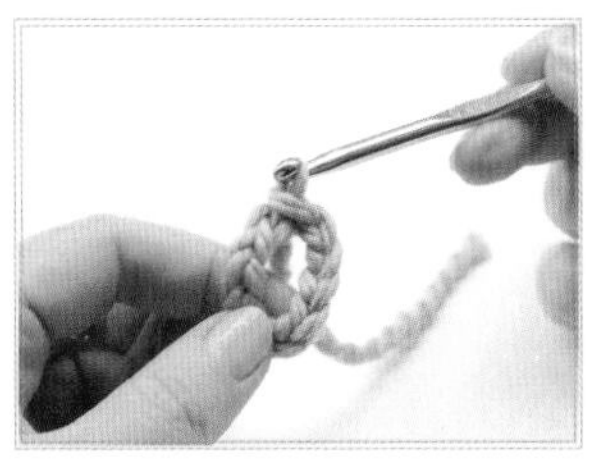

2 Insert the hook into the first stitch, yarn over and slip the yarn over through the 2 loops on the hook.

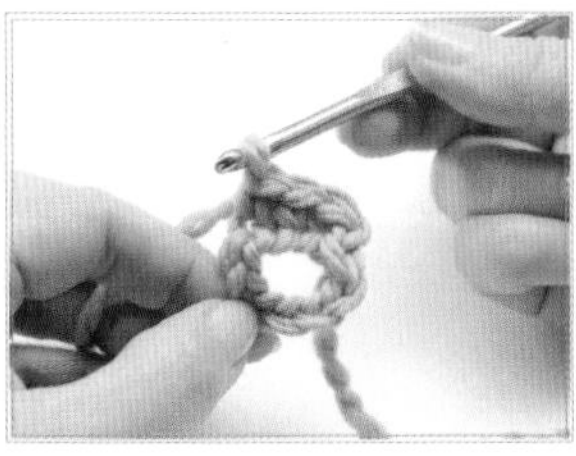

3 For rounds 1–5, ch 1 then sc 1 in each st of the chain.

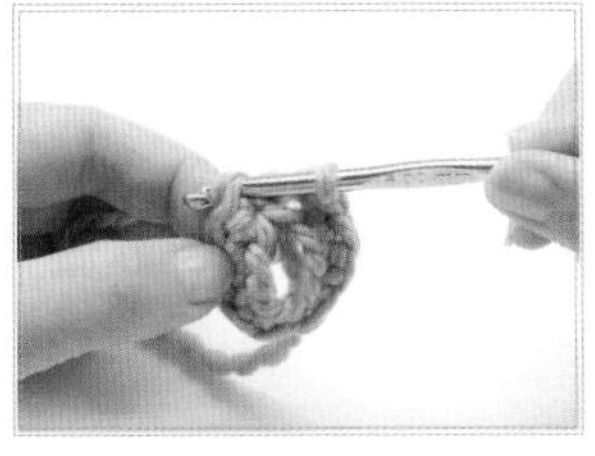

4 End each round with 1 slip stitch inserted into the ch st from the beginning of the work.

5 On round 6, ch 1, ⋆skip 1 stitch then sc 1 in the next stitch⋆.

6 Repeat from ⋆ to ⋆ 4 times total across the row.

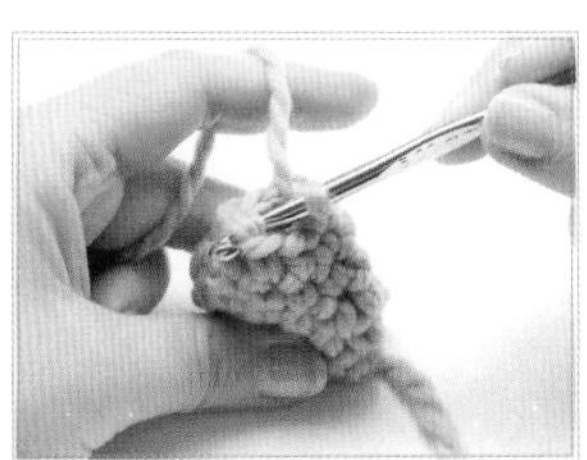

7 In order to close the thumb, put the hook under the stitch on the opposite end. Yarn over and pull the yarn over through the 2 loops on the hook. Cut the yarn.

4/ assemble the mittens and thumbs

Fold the mittens in half, right sides together. Lay the tops over each other and pin the edges, then sew a seam with back stitch (p. 67). Place the thumbs on the mittens and sew their bases with back stitch around the opening available on each mitten. Weave in the ends. Turn the mittens so the right side faces out.

CHAPTER 2

lesson 11

DECREASES AND INCREASES

LESSON 11

SAND STITCH

project: make a pair of slippers*

directions → page 112–113 • assembly → page 113 • template → page 114

MATERIALS

1 skein of fingering weight yarn, 70% wool, 30% linen, 200 yd (180m), 1¾ (50g), in burgundy (1)

11¾" x 9¾" (30cm x 25cm) of wool felt, to match yarn color

Size E-4 (3mm) crochet hook

Yarn needle

Sewing thread, to match yarn color

Sewing needle

White tailor's chalk

Scissors

Straight pins

STITCH USED

Sand stitch

SIZES

Medium, Large (to fit shoe sizes 6½–7½ / 8½–9)

GAUGE

21 stitches = 4" (10cm) wide

12 rows = 4" (10cm) high

DIMENSIONS

8¾"–10¼" long (22cm–26cm)

* In this lesson you will also learn how to sew a crocheted piece to a piece of fabric.

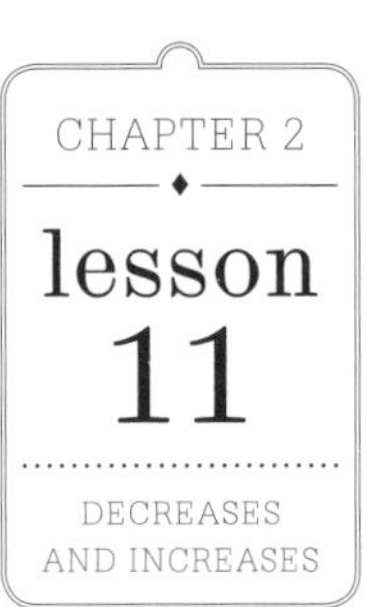

1/ make a band in sand stitch

→ **WORD OF ADVICE!**
This crocheted band forms the top of the slipper.

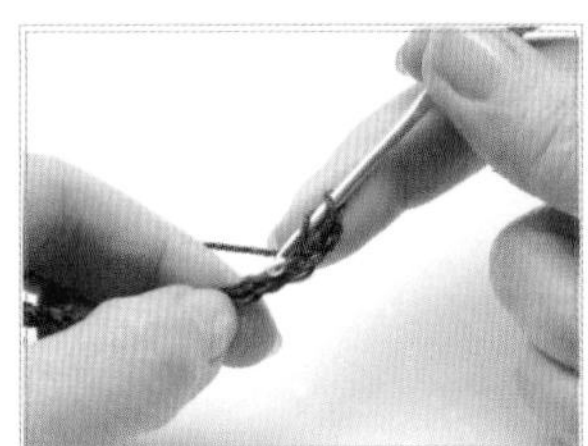

1 Make a chain of 16 sts. For row 1, on the right side of the work, dc 1 in the 4th stitch from the hook.

2 Dc 1 in each ch st from the row. End with dc 1 in the last ch st.

3 For row 2, ch 1 to turn.

4 Dc 1 twice in the first stitch of the row.

5 Skip 2 stitches.

6 Sc 1 and dc 2 all into the next stitch, skip 2 stitches.

7 Repeat step 6 three more times, then sc 1 in the 3rd ch st from the beginning of the previous row.

8 For row 3, ch 3 to turn, then sc 1 in each of the stitches in the row. Continue by repeating rows 2 and 3. Make 2 bands of sand stitch of 67 rows, measuring 16½" x 2½" (42cm x 6.5cm), for size Medium. For size Large, work 71 rows, measuring 18¼" x 2½" (46cm x 6.5cm).

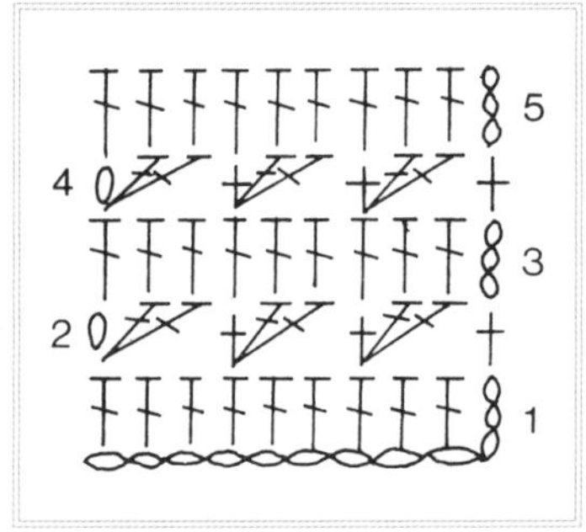

✻ **sand stitch**

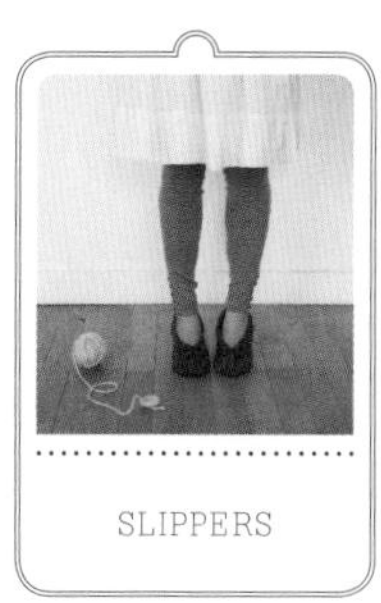

2/ make the sole of the slipper

→ WORD OF ADVICE!
Turn the template over in order to make the opposite foot.

Photocopy the template (p. 114) at 175% and cut it out. Place the template on the felt and pin. Trace the outline with the help of the tailor's pencil. Cut it out along the traced edge.

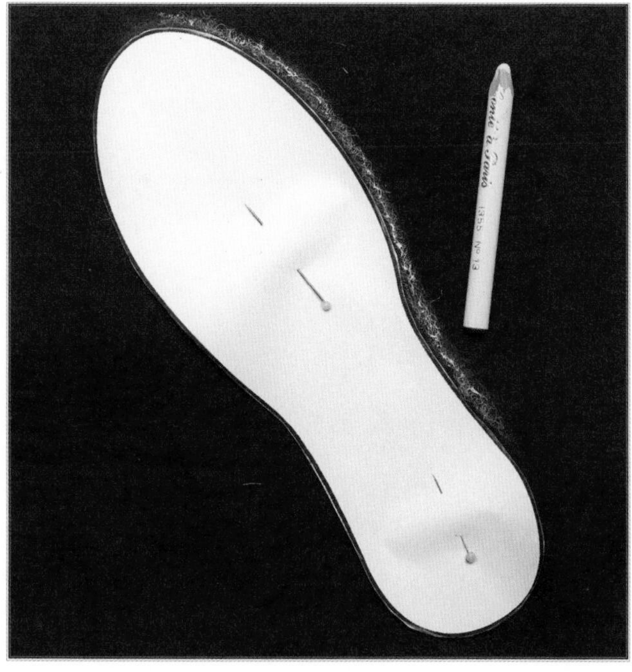

3/ assemble the slippers

→ WORD OF ADVICE!
The right slipper is assembled in the same way as the left slipper.

1 Fold the strip in half, right side to right side. Sew the widths with a back stitch (p. 68).

2 Turn over. Place the seam where your heel would be on top of your sole, and lay the edge of the strip on the outline of the sole. Pin.

3 Sew the strip and the sole with backstitch using sewing thread and a sewing needle.

4 Prepare a cord (see lesson 9, p. 96). With the yarn needle, weave the cord around the top of the strip, near the edge. Tighten and make a bow at the front of the slipper.

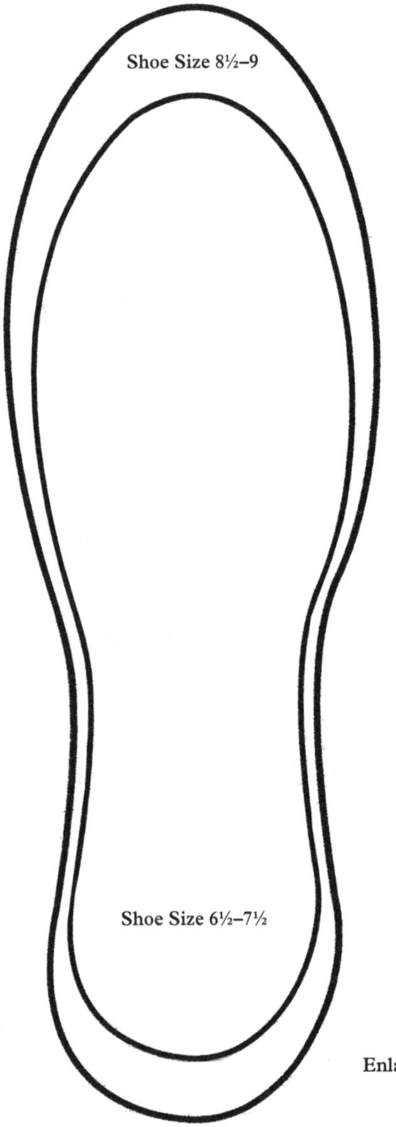

Shoe Size 8½–9

Shoe Size 6½–7½

Enlarge by 175%

CHAPTER 2

lesson 12

DECREASES AND INCREASES

LESSON 12

U-NECKLINE

project: making a kimono cardigan*

directions → page 118–120 • assembly → page 121 • schematic → page 121

MATERIALS

10 skeins of sportweight yarn,
70% wool, 30% linen, 200 yd (180m),
1¾ oz (50g) in marled brown for size Small
or 12 skeins for sizes Medium and Large (2)

Size H-8 (5mm) crochet hook

Yarn needle

1 button, ¾" (2cm)

Scissors

Straight pins

STITCHES USED

Single crochet

Diagonal ridge stitch

SIZES

Small, Medium, Large

GAUGE

For diagonal ridge stitch worked
with 2 strands

16 stitches = 4" (10cm) wide

15 rows = 4" (10cm) high

DIMENSIONS

36½", 39¼", 42¾" circumference at bust
(92.5cm, 99.5cm, 108.5cm)

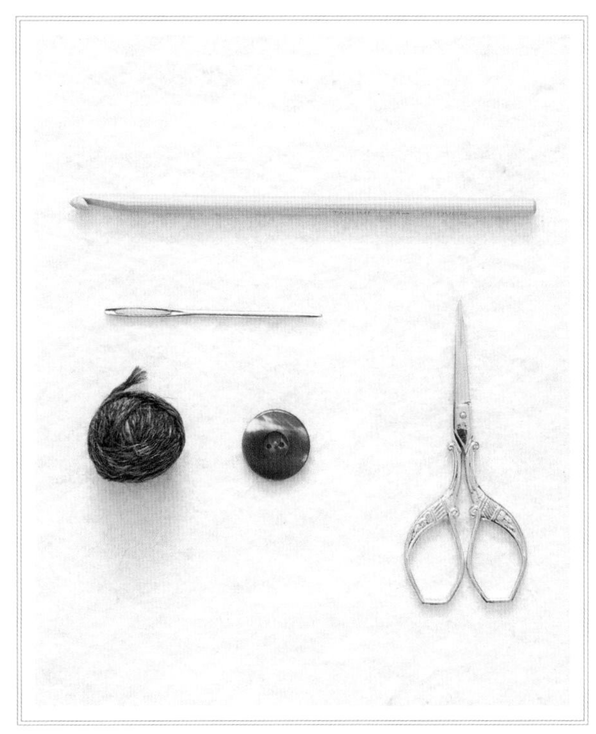

* In this lesson you will also learn how to make a neckline by using decreases and increases.

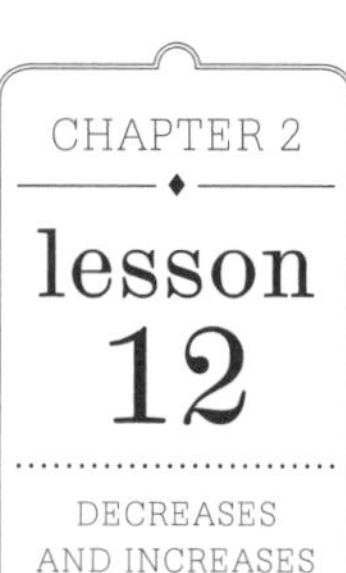

1/ starting the front for size small

1 Make a chain of 62 sts + 2 ch st, with yarn held double. Start row 1 (right side of the work) by working sc 1 in the 2nd ch st from the hook.

2 Continue the row by working sc 1 in each of the following ch sts.

3 For row 2, ch 1, sc 1 in the first sc.

4 Work *tc 1, sc 1, tc 1, sc 1 in each of the next 3 sts*. Repeat from * to * and end with sc 1 in each of the last 4 sts of the row.

5 Start rows 3 and 5 by doing ch 1, then sc 1 in the first sc.

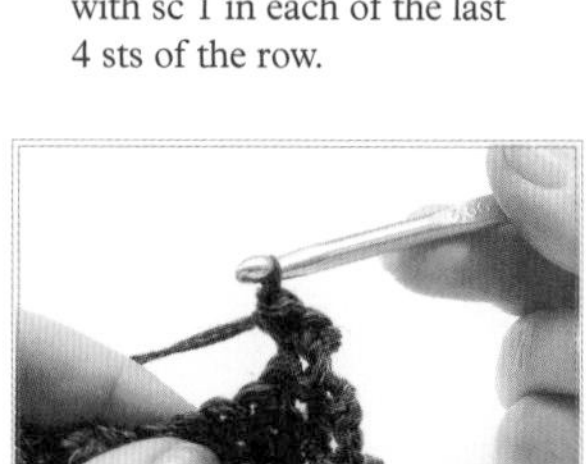

6 Continue rows 3 and 5 all in sc.

7 For row 4, ch 1, sc 1 in each of the first 2 sts, *tc 1, sc 1, tc 1, sc 3*. Repeat from * to * across the whole row. For row 6, ch 1, sc 1 in each of the first 3 sts, *tc 1, sc 1, tc 1, sc 3*. Repeat from * to * and end with sc 1 in each of the last 2 sts of the row.

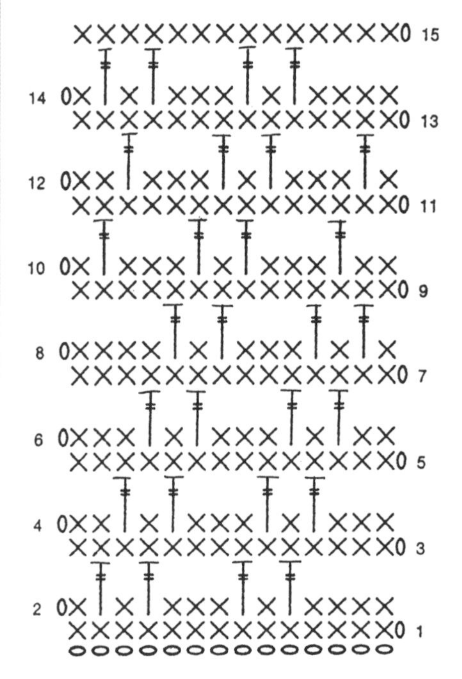

✻ **diagonal ridge stitch**

→ **ATTENTION !**

Continue the work by moving each pair of treble crochets to the left on every even row.

For rows 7–49, work even in diagonal ridge stitch

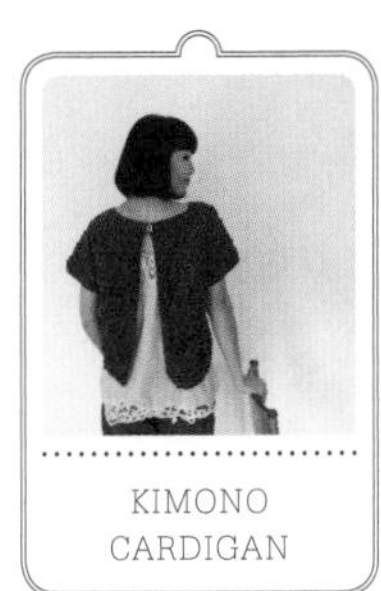
KIMONO CARDIGAN

2/ making the armholes for size small

For rows 50 and 51, make an increase: sc 2 in the first st at the beginning of the row and, likewise, sc 2 in the last st of the row. At the end of row 51, there are 66 sts.
For row 52, continue in diagonal ridge stitch and, at the end of the row, add a chain of 12 sts. There are 78 sts total.
For row 53, ch 1, continue in diagonal ridge stitch, then work the second armhole as the first by adding 12 sts. There are 90 sts total. The increased sides will form the sleeves (see diagram p. 121).

3/ make the sleeves and the neck for size small

1 For rows 54–64, continue even in diagonal ridge stitch.

2 On row 65, for the neckline, only work the 34 sts from the first sleeve. Work 4 rows in diagonal ridge stitch.

3 At the end of row 69, make a chain of 13 sts to extend the neckline.

4 Work back across the 13 sts in diagonal ridge stitch and continue on the 24 sts of the sleeve to form the side of the cardigan. There are 47 sts total. For rows 70–80, continue working even in diagonal ridge stitch.

5 For row 81, decrease 12 stitches for the armhole by leaving 12 stitches unworked. There are 35 sts. Work in diagonal ridge stitch.

6 For rows 83 and 85, from the side of the armhole, make another decrease of 1 st as follows: do not make the last sc of the row. There are 33 sts. For rows 86–160: continue even in diagonal ridge stitch on the 33 sts. Cut the yarn at the end of row 160. For the second (right) side of the cardigan, join the yarn on row 65, leaving the 22 middle sts. Work 5 rows even on the 34 sts of the second side, then continue the work mirroring the first side.

Making the cardigan in size medium

Make a chain of 68 sts + 2 sts and work as for size Small until row 51. There are 72 sts total.
For row 52: Continue in diagonal ridge stitch and, at the end of the row, add a chain of 18 sts. There are 90 sts total.
For row 53, ch 1, continue in diagonal ridge stitch then make a second armhole same as the first one by adding 18 sts to the end of the row. There are 108 sts total.
For rows 54–66: Work even in diagonal ridge stitch.
For row 67, make the neckline as follows: Only work on the first 42 stitches to make the first sleeve. Work 6 rows in diagonal ridge stitch.
For row 73: At the end of the row, add a chain of 15 sts on the neckline edge. There are 57 sts total.
For rows 74–86: Continue to work even in diagonal ridge stitch.
For row 87: Make a decrease of 18 sts on the armhole edge by leaving 18 sts unworked. There are 39 sts. Continue in diagonal ridge stitch.
For rows 89 and 91, on the armhole edge, make another decrease of 1 st as follows: do not work the last sc of the row. There are 37 sts total.
For rows 92–142: Continue even in diagonal ridge stitch on the 37 sts total. Cut the yarn at the end of row 142.

For the second side of the cardigan, join the yarn on row 67. Work 6 rows even on the 42 sts of the second side, leaving the middle 24 sts, then continue the work mirroring the other side.

Making the cardigan for size large

Make a chain of 74 sts + 2 sts and work as for size Small until row 51. There are 78 sts total.
For row 52: Continue in diagonal ridge stitch and, at the end of the row, add a chain of 18 sts. There are 96 sts total.
For row 53: Ch 1, continue in diagonal ridge stitch then make the second armhole as for the first by adding 18 sts to the end of the row. There are 114 sts total.
For rows 54–66: Continue even in diagonal ridge stitch.
For row 67, make the neckline as follows: Only work on the first 44 sts to make the first sleeve. Work 6 rows in diagonal ridge stitch.
For row 73: At the end of the row, add a chain of 15 sts to the neck side. There are 59 sts total.
For rows 74–86: Continue even in diagonal ridge stitch.
For row 87: Make a decrease of 18 sts on the armhole edge by leaving 18 sts unworked. There are 41 sts. Continue in diagonal ridge stitch.
For rows 89 and 91, from the armhole edge, make another decrease of 1 st as follows: Do not work the last sc of the row. There are 39 sts total.
For rows 92–142: Continue even in diagonal ridge stitch on the 39 sts. Cut the yarn at the end of row 142.

For the second side of the cardigan, join the yarn to row 67. Work 6 rows even on the 44 sts of the second side, leaving the 26 middle sts, then continue the work mirroring the other side.

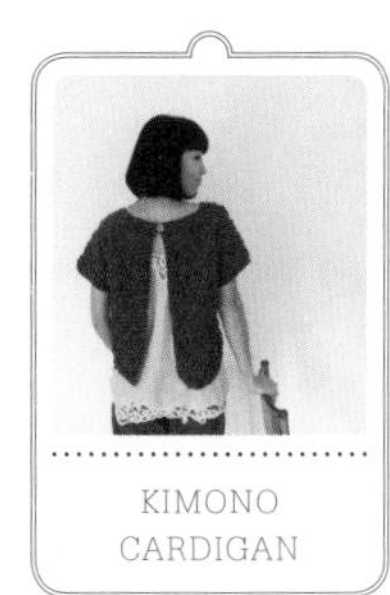

4/ sew the cardigan

→ **ATTENTION!**
Before sewing the cardigan, weave in your ends. Fold the piece in half at the shoulders and sew the edge of the sleeves with a backstitch (p. 68). Assemble the sides and the back in the same way. Make a buttonhole on one of the sides of the cardigan at the top.

1 In order to make the buttonhole, join the yarn with a slip stitch at the top of the right side of the cardigan.

2 Make a chain of 5 sts.

3 Slip stitch 1, ½" (13mm) down from the top of the piece. Sew the button on the other side at the same spot.

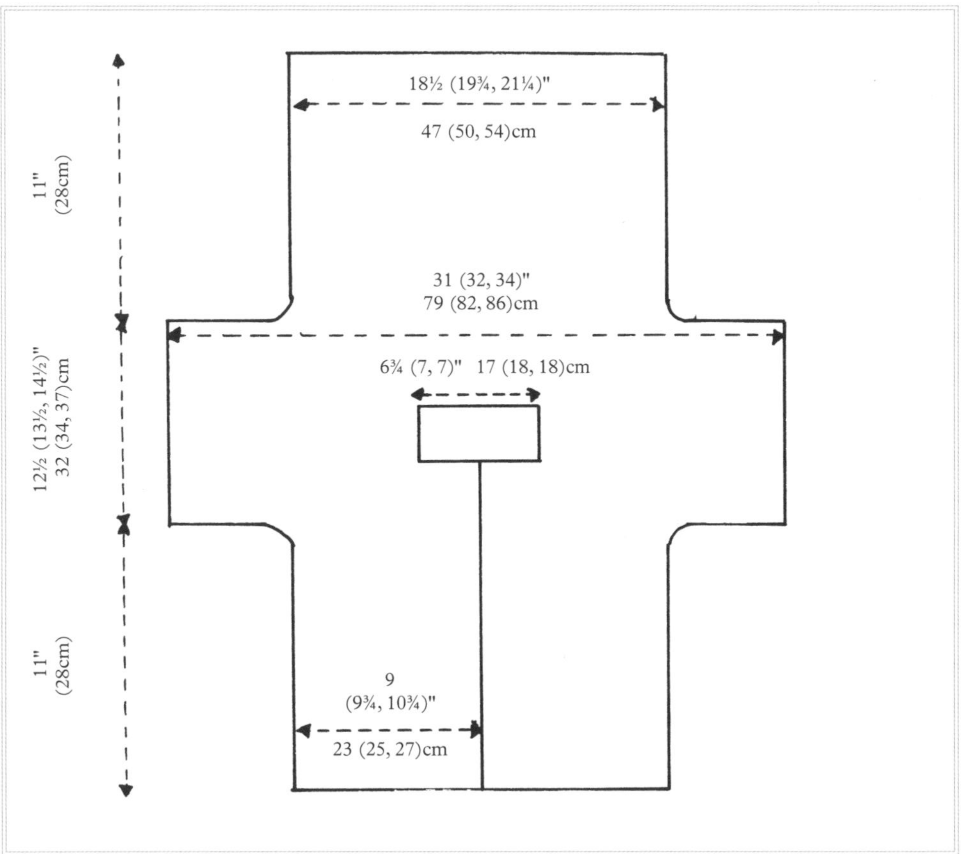

CHAPTER 2

lesson 13

DECREASES AND INCREASES

LESSON 13

REVERSIBLE STITCH

project: making a sleeveless pullover*

directions → page 124–127 • schematic → page 126 • assembly → page 127

MATERIALS

13 skeins of bulky yarn, 100% wool, 55yd (50m), 1¾ oz (50g) for size Small

or 14 skeins for size Medium

or 16 skeins for size Large (5)

Size J-10 (6mm) crochet hook

Yarn needle

Scissors

STITCH USED

Croissant stitch

SIZE

Small, Medium, and Large

GAUGE

13 stitches = 4" (10cm) wide

6 rows = 4" (10cm) high

DIMENSIONS

33", 37", and 39¾" bust circumference (84cm, 94cm, and 101cm)

* In this lesson you will also learn how to make a turtleneck.

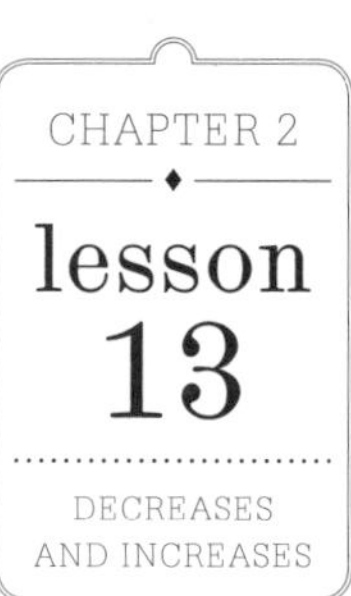

1/ make the back and the front for size Small

→ **WORD OF ADVICE!**
For sizes Medium and Large, refer to the directions on page 127 for the number of stitches.

1 Make a chain of 51 sts (6 croissant motifs). For row 1, ch 3 (=1 dc) + ch 1, skip 4 ch sts.

2 Dc 3 into the next stitch, ch 1.

3 Dc 3 into the stitch before the one where the dc 3 was just worked.

4 Ch 1.

5 Skip 3 stitches, sc 1, ch 1, skip 4 sts.

6 Repeat steps 2–5 across the row.

7 End the row with dc 3 in the next stitch.

8 Ch 1, sc 3 in the preceding stitch, ch 1, skip 3 sts, dc 1 in the last ch st.

9 Start row 2 with ch 3, dc 3 in the last ch st of the previous row.

10 Continue with ch 1, sc 1 in the ch st between the 2 groups of dc.

11 Next, ch 1, dc 3 in the ch st after the sc.

12 Finish the stitch with ch 1, dc 3 in the st before the sc.

13 Repeat steps 10–12 across the row. End with ch 1, sc 1, ch 1, dc 3 in the ch st.

14 Dc 1 in the 3rd ch st from the previous row.

15 For row 3, ch 3 (= 1 dc) + ch 1, *dc 3 in the ch st after the sc, ch 1, sc 3 in the ch st before the sc, ch 1, sc 1 in the ch st between the 2 groups of 3 dc, ch 1*. Repeat from * to * across the row. End with dc 3 in the ch st after the sc, ch 1, dc 3 in the ch st before the sc, ch 1, dc 1. Continue the work by repeating rows 2 and 3.

Work even for 20 rows of croissant stitch = 13" (33cm).

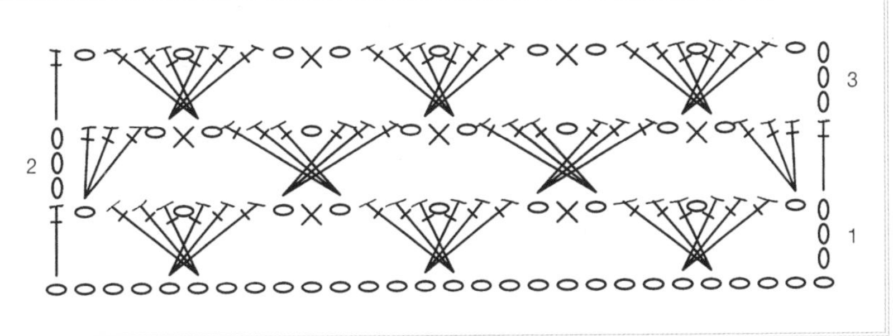

✻ **croissant stitch**

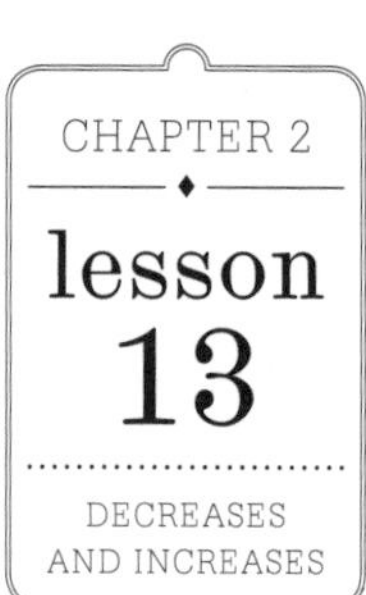

2/ shape the armholes and the neck

→ **WORD OF ADVICE!**
The armholes and the neck are shaped by making decreases.

To make the armholes, on row 22, decrease 5 sts at each end of the row. The piece will continue over the middle 41 sts (= 4½ croissant motifs). Continue even for 14 rows of croissant motifs = 8½" (22 cm). When the piece measures 21½" (55cm), shape the shoulders by decreasing 3 sts at each end of the row. The piece will continue over the middle 35 sts (= 3 croissant motifs). Work another 9 rows = 6" (15cm) in croissant stitch to make the turtleneck. At 27½" (70cm), break the yarn.

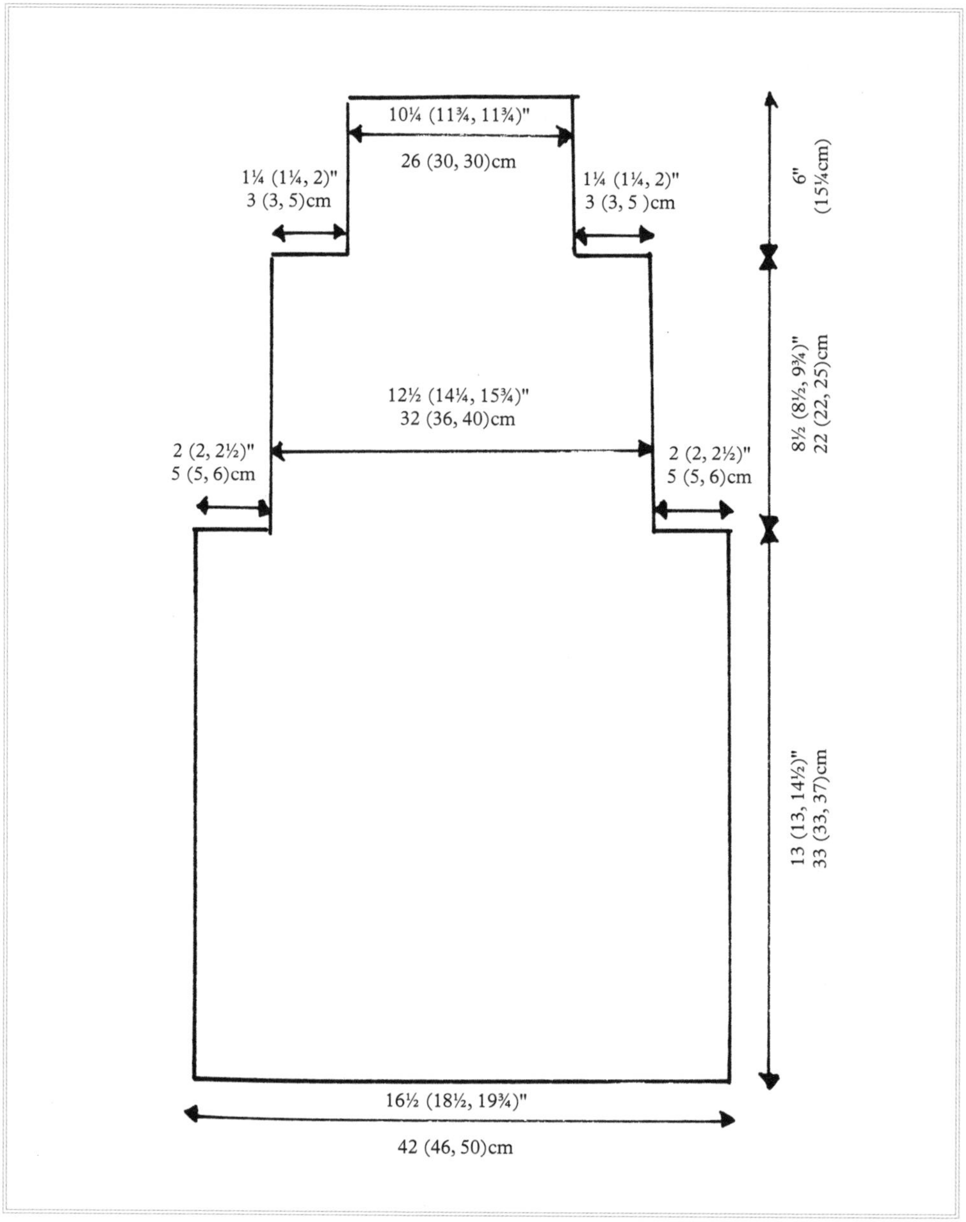

10¼ (11¾, 11¾)"
26 (30, 30)cm

1¼ (1¼, 2)"
3 (3, 5)cm

1¼ (1¼, 2)"
3 (3, 5)cm

6"
(15¼cm)

12½ (14¼, 15¾)"
32 (36, 40)cm

2 (2, 2½)"
5 (5, 6)cm

2 (2, 2½)"
5 (5, 6)cm

8½ (8½, 9¾)"
22 (22, 25)cm

13 (13, 14½)"
33 (33, 37)cm

16½ (18½, 19¾)"
42 (46, 50)cm

3/ sew the sleeveless top

→ **DON'T FORGET !**
Weave in your ends before starting to sew the sleeveless top.

Place the front and the back on top of each other, right sides together. Pin. Assemble with backstitch (see p. 68) using the same yarn as the crocheted garment.

For size medium

1 **Make the back and the front**

Make a chain of 60 sts (= 7 croissant motifs) and work as for size Small.
Work even for 20 rows of the croissant motifs, or 13" (33cm).

2 **Shape the armholes and the neck**

→ **WORD OF ADVICE!**
The armholes and the neck are shaped by only making decreases.

To make the armholes, on row 22, decrease 5 sts at each end of the row. The piece will continue over the middle 50 sts (= 5½ croissant motifs).
Continue even for 14 rows of the croissant motifs, or 8½" (22cm).
When the piece measures 21½ (55cm), shape the shoulders by decreasing 3 sts at each end of the row. The piece will continue over the middle 44 sts (= 4 croissant motifs). Work 9 more rows, or 6" (15cm) in croissant stitch to make the turtleneck.
At 27½" (70cm), break the yarn.

For size large

1 **Make the back and the front**

Make a chain of 69 sts (= 8 croissant motifs) and work as for size Small.
Work even for 21 rows of the croissant motifs, or 14½" (37cm).

2 **Shape the armholes and the neck**

→ **WORD OF ADVICE!**
The armholes and the neck are shaped by making decreases.

To shape the armholes, on row 23, decrease 7 sts at each end of the row. The work will continue over the middle 55 sts (= 6 croissant motifs).
Continue even for 15 rows of the croissant motifs, or 9¾" (25cm).
When the piece measures 24½" (62cm), shape the shoulders by decreasing 5 sts at each end of the row. The work will continue over the middle 45 sts (= 5 croissant motifs). Work another 9 rows, or 6" (15cm) in croissant stitch to make the turtleneck.
At 30½" (77cm), break the yarn.

CHAPTER 3

STARTING LACE STITCHES

CHAPTER 3

lesson 14

STARTING LACE STITCHES

LESSON 14

FILET MESH STITCH

project 1: make a filet mesh bag

directions → pages 134–136 • schematic → page 136 • assembly → page 137 • variation → page 138

MATERIALS

3 skeins of fingering-weight yarn, 50% viscose, 45% cotton, 170 yd (156m), 2 skeins in taupe and 1 skein in sky blue (1)

Size C-2 (2.75mm) crochet hook

Yarn needle

Scissors

Straight pins

Fabric for lining (optional)

STITCHES USED

Filet mesh stitch

Single crochet

SIZE

One size

GAUGE

25 sts = 4" (10cm) wide

15 rows = 4" (10cm) high

DIMENSIONS

10½" wide x 12½" high (27cm x 32cm)

CHAPTER 3

lesson 14

STARTING LACE STITCHES

1/ make a filet mesh bag

1 Start by making the bottom of the filet bag with a chain of 72 sts using sky blue.
For rows 1–4: Ch 1 to turn and work the whole row in sc.

2 **On row 5,** change colors and work in taupe. Ch 6 to turn, skip the first 3 sc.

3 Dc 1 in the next sc.

4 *Ch 3.

5 Skip 3 sc.

6 Dc 1 in the next sc*. Repeat from * to * (from step 4 to step 6) across the whole row and end with dc 1 in the last sc of the previous row.

7 **Next row:** Continue the work from row 2 of filet mesh stitch: ch 1 to turn, sc 1 in the first stitch (the last dc of the previous row).

8 Ch 3, skip the arch from the 3 ch sts of the previous row.

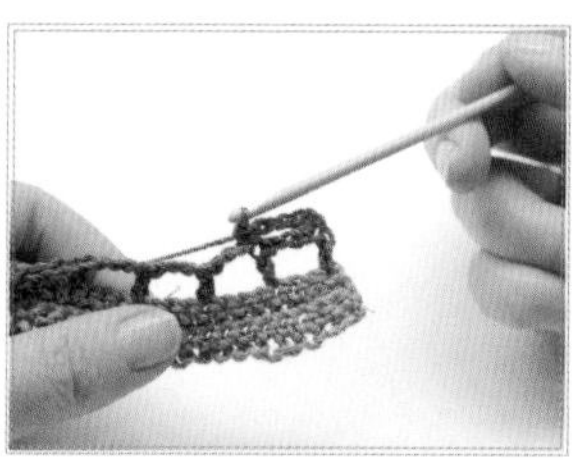

9 Sc 1 in the next dc. Repeat steps 8–9 across the row and end with sc in the 4th ch st from the beginning of row 1 of filet mesh stitch.

10 Work 7 rows in filet mesh stitch then change colors for row 12. Work in sky blue. Ch 1 to turn.

11 Work all of row 12 in sc in sky blue.

For row 13: Continue in taupe and work as for row 5.
For rows 14 and 15: Continue the work from row 2 of filet mesh stitch.
For row 16: Work as for row 12 in sky blue.
For row 17: Continue in taupe and work as for row 5.
For rows 18–31: Continue the work from row 2 of filet mesh stitch.
For row 32: Work as for row 12 in sky blue.
For row 33: Continue in taupe and work as for row 5.
For rows 34-65: Continue the work from row 2 of filet mesh stitch.
For row 66: Work as for row 12 in sky blue.
For row 67: Continue in taupe and work as for row 5.
For rows 68-81: Continue the work from row 2 of filet mesh stitch.
For row 82: Work as for row 12 in sky blue.
For row 83: Continue in taupe and work as for row 5.
For rows 84 and 85: Continue the work from row 2 of filet mesh stitch.
For row 86: Work as for row 12 in sky blue.
For row 87: Continue in taupe and work as for row 5.
For rows 8–93: Continue the work from row 2 of filet mesh stitch.
For rows 94–98: Change colors. Continuing in sky blue, ch 1 and work the whole row in sc. Continue the rows with sc.
End and cut the yarn at the end of row 102.

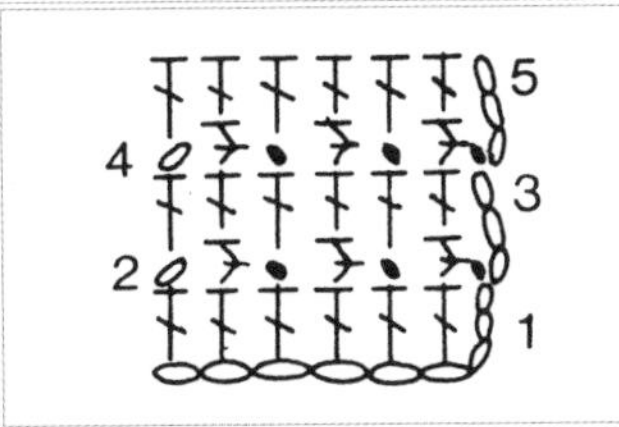

* **filet mesh stitch**

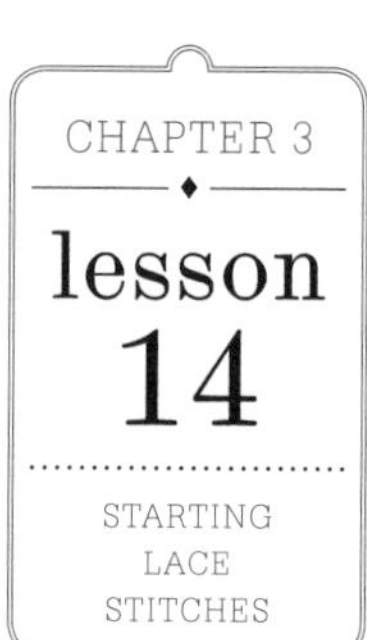

2/ make the handles

In sky blue, make a chain of 98 sts or 15¾" (40cm).
For rows 1–5: Ch 1 to turn and work the whole row in sc. Stop and cut the yarn at the end of row 5. Make a second handle the same way.

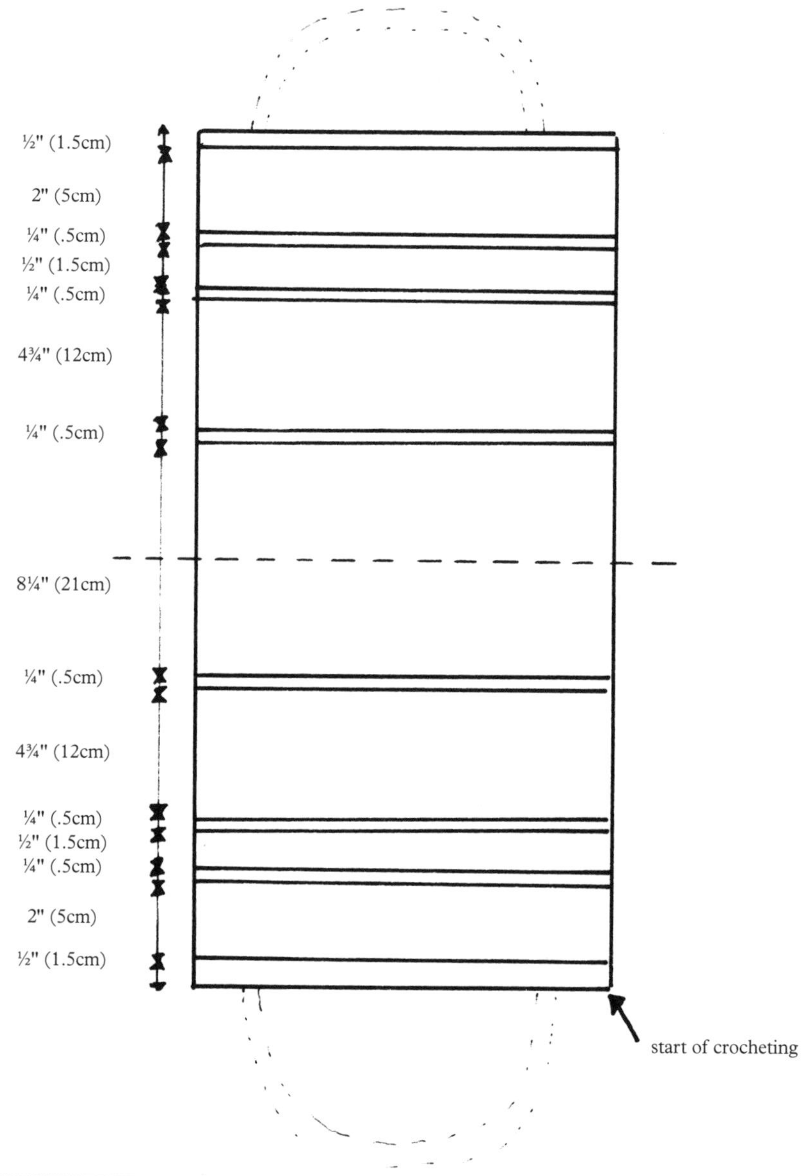

½" (1.5cm)
2" (5cm)
¼" (.5cm)
½" (1.5cm)
¼" (.5cm)
4¾" (12cm)
¼" (.5cm)
8¼" (21cm)
¼" (.5cm)
4¾" (12cm)
¼" (.5cm)
½" (1.5cm)
¼" (.5cm)
2" (5cm)
½" (1.5cm)
start of crocheting

FILET BAG

3/ assemble the filet bag

→ DON'T FORGET!
Weave in your ends before assembling the bag.

1 Fold the rectangle in half to make a rectangle 10½" (27cm) wide by 12½" (32cm) high. Pin and sew with a backstitch (p. 68). Turn the bag so the right-side is facing out.

2 Position the ends of the handles on the sc border, 2½ (6.5cm) from the sides, so that the bottoms of the handles are at the bottom of the border. Pin, then sew with backstitch.

→ LINING THE BAG

This bag is very practical for transporting bulky groceries or other items. To conceal or transport smaller objects, you should add a lining. Choose a solid or print cotton cloth, such as Liberty-style lawn, and cut a rectangle with the same dimensions as the crocheted rectangle, adding ¾" (2cm) to the width and ½" (13mm) to the length. Fold the two short sides over twice by ½" (13mm), and sew ¼" (6mm) from the edge. Sew the two long sides. Fold the lining in two, wrong sides together, and sew the sides ½" (13mm) from the edge. Put the lining inside the bag and sew the top to the top of the bag by hand with short slip stitches.

project 2: the filet mesh scarf

MATERIALS

4 skeins of sportweight yarn, 51% wool, 49% kid mohair, 280 yd (255m), 1¾ oz (50g), in pastel pink (2)

Size E-4 (3.5mm) crochet hook

Yarn needle

SIZE

One size

DIMENSIONS

15" x 63" (38cm x 160cm)

DIRECTIONS

This stitch is useful for all kinds of projects—for example, this cozy, oversized scarf. For a big scarf, make a chain of 61 sts with one strand of the mohair and work in filet mesh stitch with the size E-4 (3.5mm) crochet hook. At 63" (160cm), cut the yarn and weave in your ends.

CHAPTER 3

lesson 15

STARTING LACE STITCHES

LESSON 15

STARTING LACE STITCHES

project 1: make a pair of fingerless mittens*

directions → pages 142–143 • assembly → page 144 • schematic → page 145 • variation → page 146

MATERIALS

2 skeins of fingering-weight yarn, 51% pure wool, 49% kid mohair, 280 yd (255m), 1¾ oz (50g), in bronze (1)

Size E-4 (3.5mm) crochet hook

Size D-3 (3.25mm) crochet hook

Yarn needle

Scissors

Straight pins

STITCHES USED

Open-work stitch

Double crochet

SIZE

One size

GAUGE FOR THE OPEN-WORK STITCH

30 sts = 4" (10cm) wide

13 rows = 4" (10cm) high

DIMENSIONS

9" (11cm) in circumference.
13¾" (35cm) long

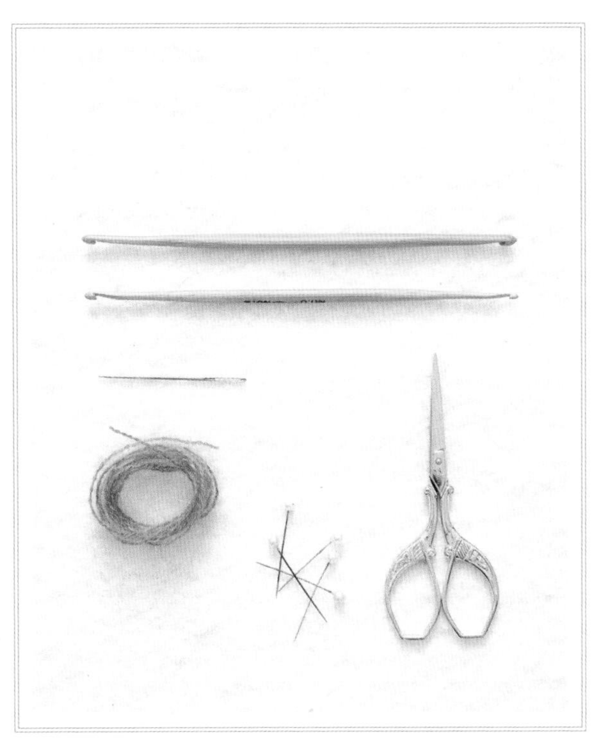

* You will also learn in this lesson how to make the matching fringed scarf.

1/ make the fingerless mittens

→ **WORD OF ADVICE!**
The piece starts at the top of the forearm.

1 With the E-4 (3.5mm) hook, make a chain of 57 + 2 sts. **For row 1** (wrong side of the piece), ch 3, skip 1 st and work 1 single V motif in the next stitch: dc 1, ch 1, dc 1.

2 Skip 2 ch sts.

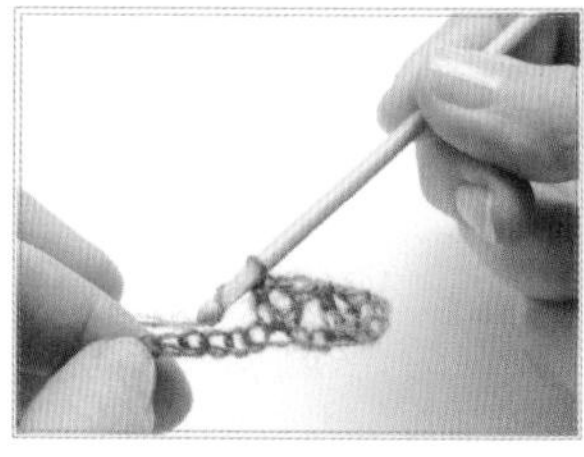

3 Work 1 single V motif in the next ch st [dc 1, ch 1, dc 1]. Repeat steps 2 and 3 across the row.

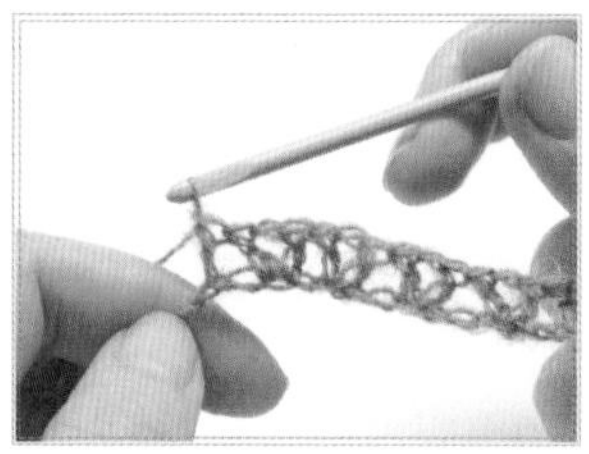

4 End the row by skipping 1 ch st and working dc 1 in the last ch st of the row.

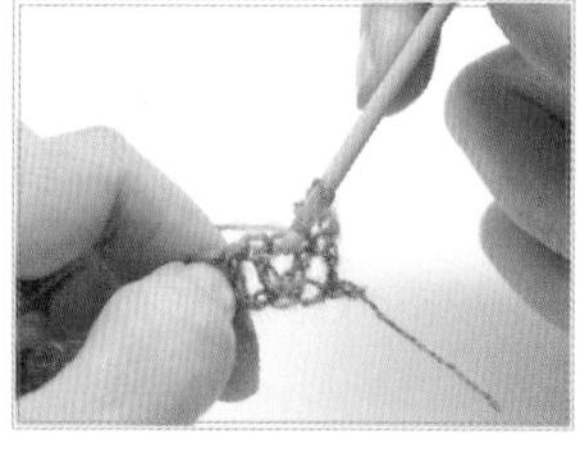

5 **For row 2,** ch 3, skip 1 st and work 1 double V motif: dc 2 in the arc of the ch from row 1.

6 Ch 1.

7 Dc 2 in the same arc. Steps 5–7 produce 1 double V motif [dc 2, ch 1, dc2].

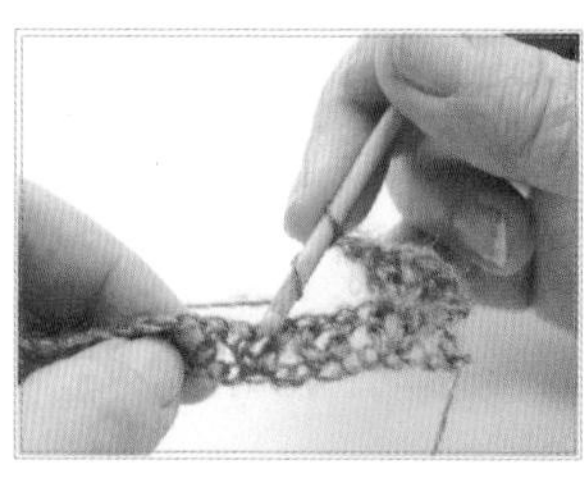

8 Ch 1, skip the next single V motif, work 1 double V motif in the arc of the next ch.

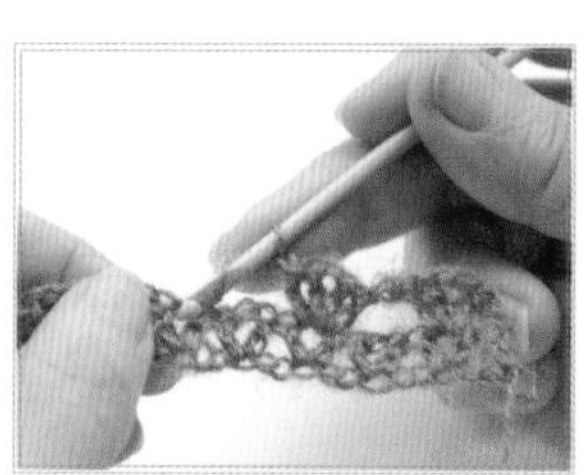

9 Repeat step 8 across the row. On the last double V motif, work dc2tog as follows: begin with the beginning of the last dc from the V motif, then insert the hook into the last st of the row and make the 2nd dc of the dc2tog.

10 **For row 3,** begin with a ch 3.

11 Then work 1 single V motif [dc 1, ch 1, dc 1] in each arc of the ch 1 from the previous row.

12 End row 3 with dc 1 in the last dc of the previous row.

13 **For row 4,** work *ch 3, dc 1 in the first st, ch 1, and skip the first single V motif of the previous row. Work 1 double V motif [dc 2, ch 1, dc 2] in the next arc, ch 1, skip the next single V motif*.

14 Repeat from * to * and end with dc 2 in the 3rd ch st from the beginning of the previous row.
For row 5, repeat row 3.
From row 6 to row 29: Continue in open-work stitch, repeating rows 3 and 4.

15 **For row 30,** take the D-3 (3.25mm) hook. Ch 2, skip the first st, *work 1 hdc in the next 5 sts, skip the next ch st (the ch st between 2 V motifs)* and continue from * to * across the row. There are 50 hdc.
For rows 31–39: ch 2 to turn, then hdc 1 in each st of the row.
For row 40: Continue the work with open-work Stitch with the D-3 (3.25mm) hook, skipping the first and last stitch of the row to work over 48 sts.
For rows 41–45: Work in open-work stitch. Stop at the end of row 45.

Work a second fingerless mitten in the same way.

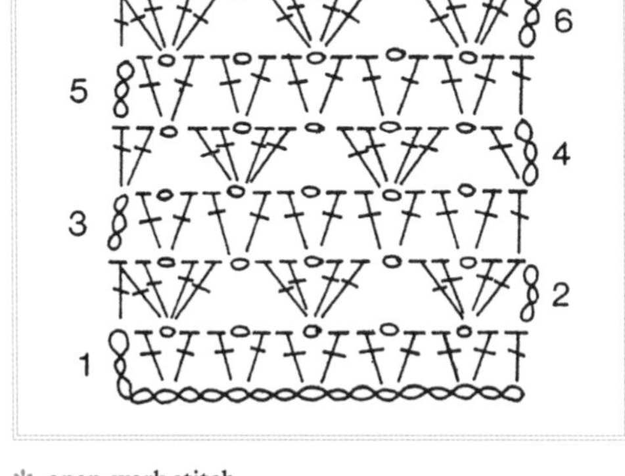

* **open-work stitch**

2/ sew the fingerless mittens

→ **WORD OF ADVICE!**
Weave in your ends before seaming.

1 Fold one fingerless mitten in half lengthwise, right sides together, and sew with backstitch (p. 68). Stop sewing right at the bottom of the section worked in hdc. This will be the thumb hole.

2 Resume sewing on the part with the open-work stitches. Turn the work so the right side is facing out. Repeat with the second fingerless mitten.

This fingerless mitten pattern can very easily be adapted to be a different length.
To have shorter mittens, begin with the same number of stitches, work 5 rows of open-work stitch motifs, then finish the mittens as indicated in the initial directions, when the piece is the length of your hand, or as desired.
To have longer mittens, work until the piece reaches right above the elbow; you should work 25 rows of open-work stitch motifs then continue the directions from row 31.

FINGERLESS
MITTENS

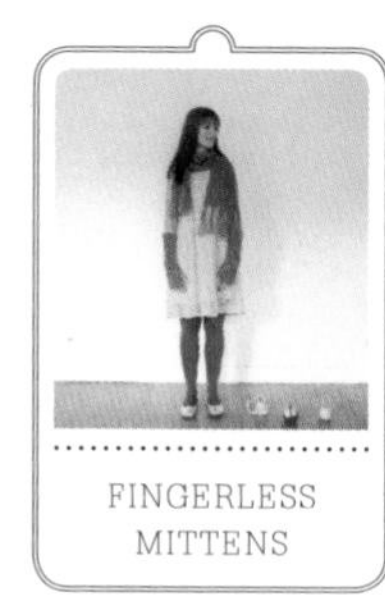

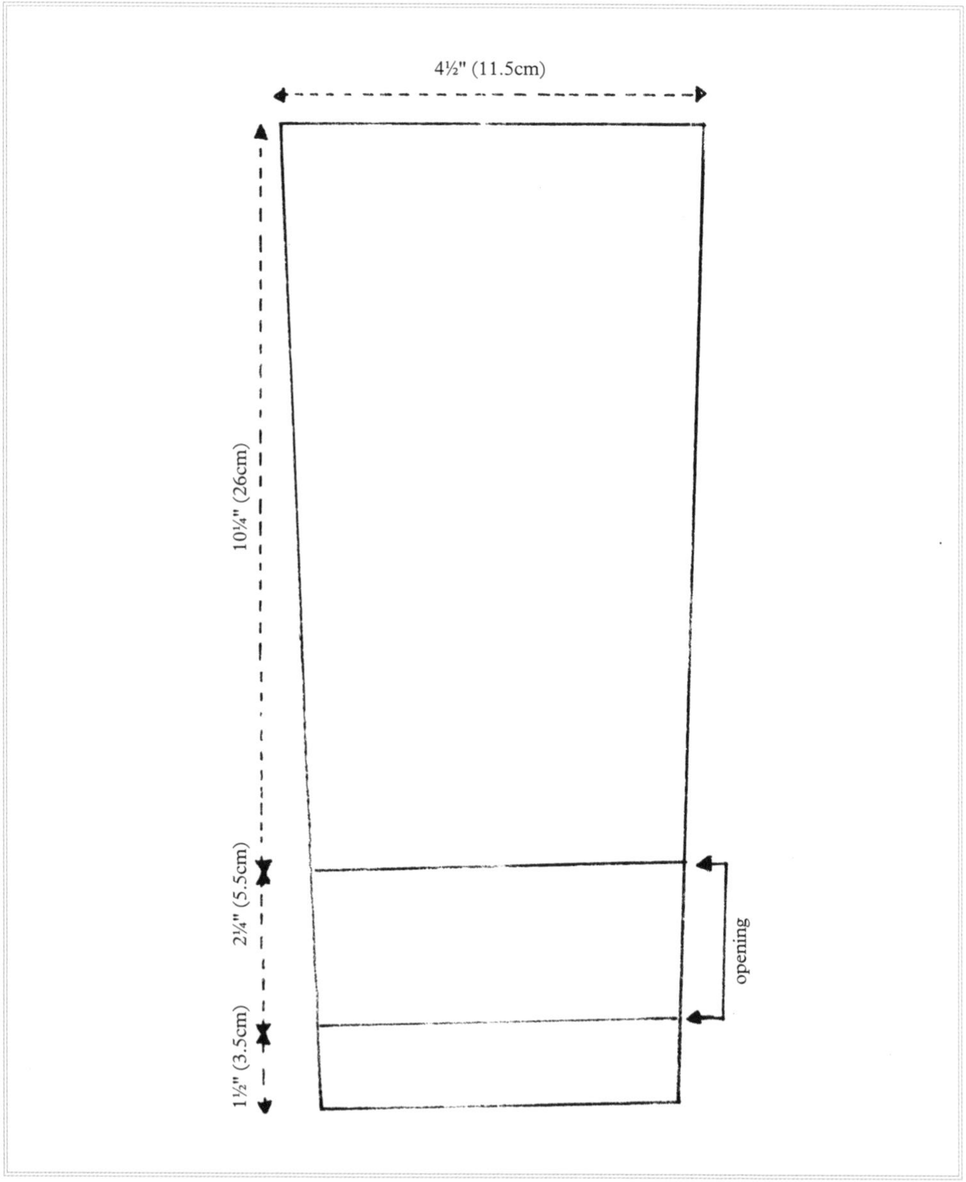

4½" (11.5cm)
10¼" (26cm)
2¼" (5.5cm)
1½" (3.5cm)
opening

✻ **schematic for sewing**

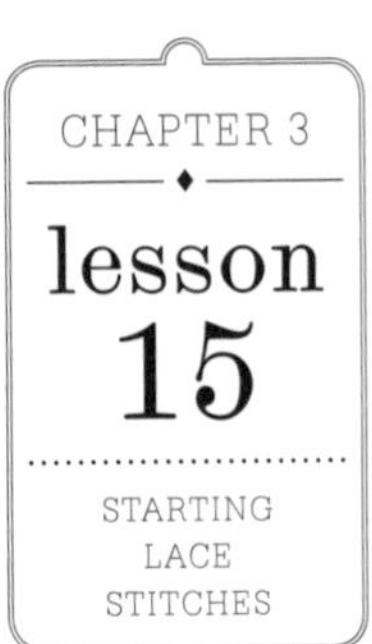

project 2: the fringed scarf

MATERIALS

5 skeins of fingering-weight yarn, 51% pure wool, 49% kid mohair, 280 yd (255m), 1¾ oz (50g), in bronze (1)

Size H-8 (5mm) crochet hook

Yarn needle

SIZE

One size

DIMENSIONS

8½" x 49" (22cm x 125cm)

DIRECTIONS

To make a thick, warm scarf to coordinate with the fingerless mittens, work with 2 strands held together. Make a chain of 37 sts and crochet for 49" (125cm) in open-work stitch (= 78 rows). Cut the yarn and weave in your ends. To make the fringe, wrap 15 strands of yarn around a piece of cardboard 7¾" (20cm) wide. Cut the yarn loop along one length of the cardboard, creating a bundle of long strands, and carefully remove it from the cardboard. Insert the folded end of the fringe into an opening in the scarf and, with the help of a crochet hook, pull the two ends of the fringe through the loop and tighten. Work fringe 13 times at each end of the scarf, spacing the fringe evenly. Even out the lengths of the fringe with scissors.

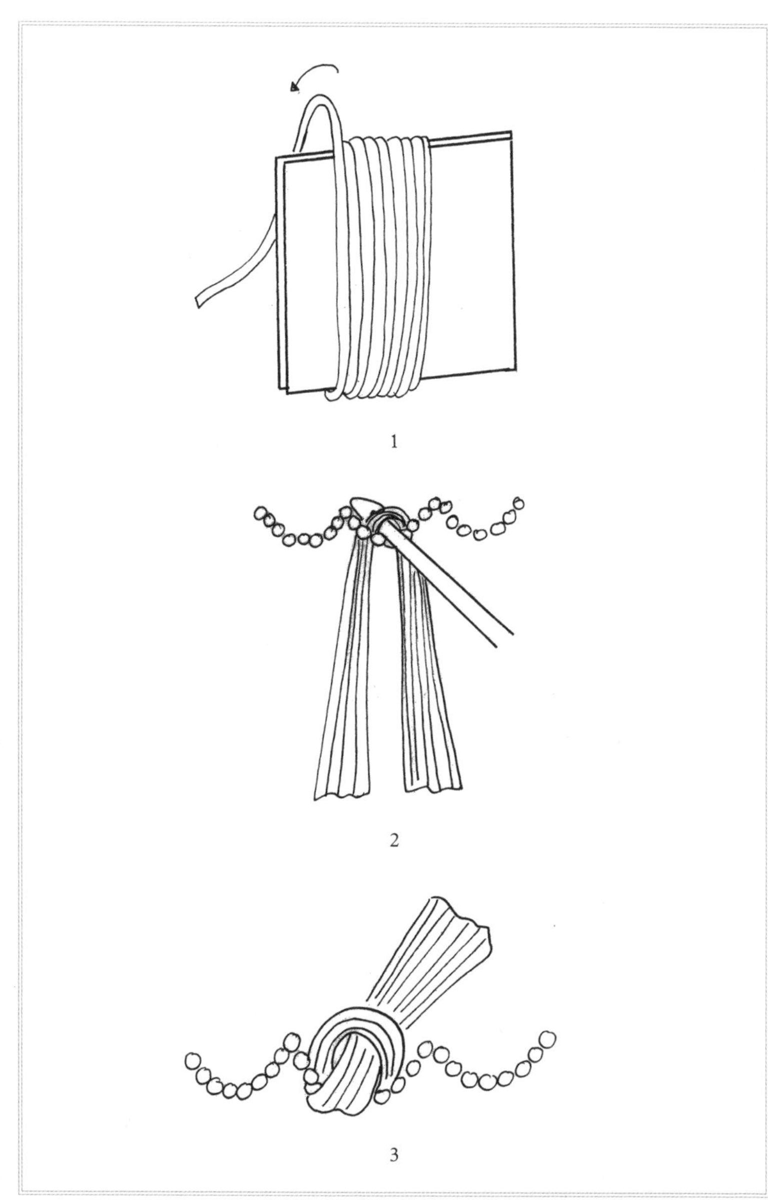

✻ **to make fringe**

CHAPTER 3

lesson 16

STARTING LACE STITCHES

LESSON 16

SHELL STITCH

project: making a large scarf*

directions → pages 150–151 • schematic → page 151

MATERIALS

15 skeins of bulky weight yarn, 100% 55yd (50m), 1¾ oz (50g), in bisque (5)

4 skeins of fingering-weight yarn, 51% pure wool, 49% kid mohair, 280 yd (255m), 1¾ oz (50g), in grape (1)

Size N-15 (10mm) crochet hook

Scissors

Yarn needle

STITCH USED

Shell stitch

SIZE

One size

GAUGE

13 sts = 4" (10cm) wide

6 rows = 4" (10cm) high

DIMENSIONS

13" x 3¼ yd (35cm x 3m)

* In this lesson you will also learn how to crochet with two different yarns at the same time.

1/ starting the scarf

→ **WORD OF ADVICE!**
The rows of the shells are worked with 1 yarn strand of bisque and 2 stands of grape together. The two rows of the arches worked using chains and single crochets are worked with only 2 strands of grape.

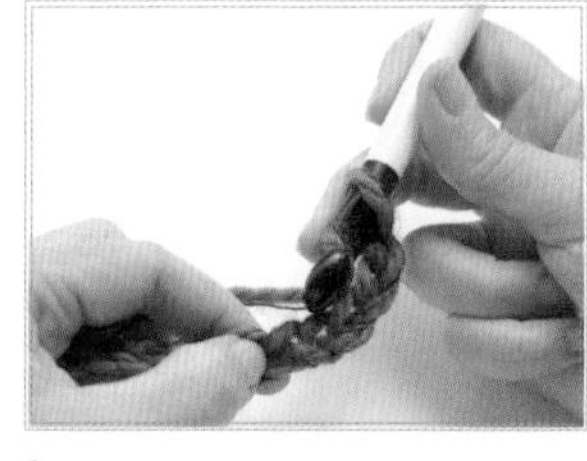

1 With the 3 strands (1 bisque + 2 grape), make a chain of 32 sts.

2 **For row 1** (with the 3 strands), ch 3, then work 1 shell of 3 dc in the 4th chain from the hook.

3 Skip 3 ch sts and *sc 1 in the next ch st.

4 Skip 3 ch sts and work 1 shell of 7 dc in the next ch st.

5 Skip 3 ch sts*. Repeat from * to * 2 more times and end the row with 1 shell of 4 dc in the last st.

6 **For row 2,** drop the strand of bisque and work with the 2 strands of grape. Ch 5.

7 Skip the shell of 4 dc from the previous row and *sc 1 in the sc of row 1, ch 3, skip the next 3 dc, sc 1 in the 4th dc of the previous row, ch 3, skip the next 3 dc*.

8 Repeat from * to * across the row and end with sc 1 in the 3rd ch st from the beginning of the previous row.

9 **For row 3** (in grape), ch 1, *sc 1 in the sc from the previous row, ch 3, skip the next arc of the 3 ch sts.

10 Sc 1 in the sc from the previous row, ch 3, skip the next arc of 3 ch sts*.

11 Repeat from * to * across the row and end with sc 1 in the 3rd ch st of the 5 ch sts from the beginning of the previous row.

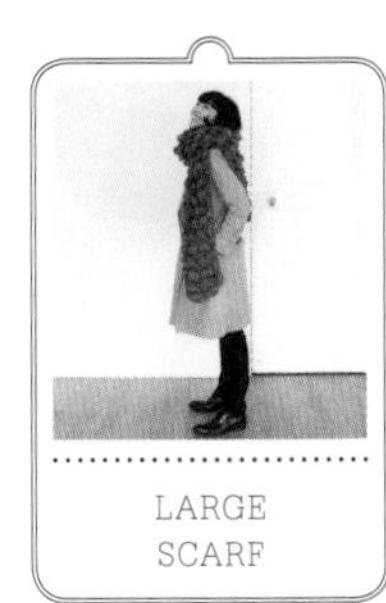

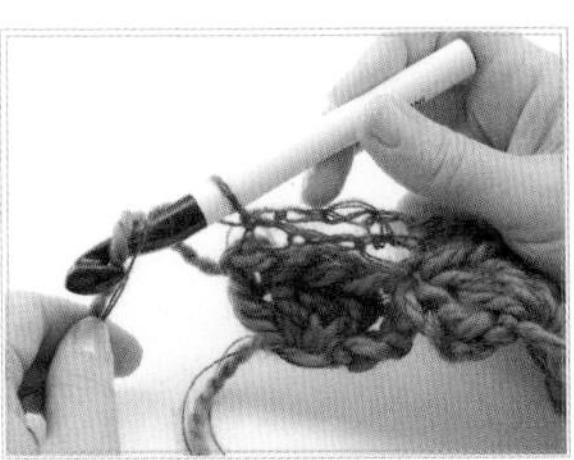

12 Pick up the strand of bisque on row 4 and with all three, pull it up through the side edge.

13 With the 3 strands, ch 1, sc 1 in the first stitch, *skip the next arc, work 1 shell of 7 dc in the next sc, skip the next arc, sc 1 in the next sc*.

14 Repeat from * to * across the row and end by sc 1 in the last sc of the previous row.

2/ finishing the scarf

For row 5: Work as for row 2
For row 6: Work as for row 3.
For row 7: Pick up the strand of bisque and pull it up through the side edge. With the 3 strands, ch 3 to turn, work 1 shell of 3 dc in the first sc of the row, skip the next arc, and *sc 1 in the next sc, skip the next arc, work a shell of 7 dc in the next sc, skip the next arc*. Repeat from * to * 2 more times and end the row with 1 shell of 4 dc in the last sc.
Repeat rows 2–7 until piece measures 3¼ yd (3m) in length. Cut the yarn and weave in your ends.

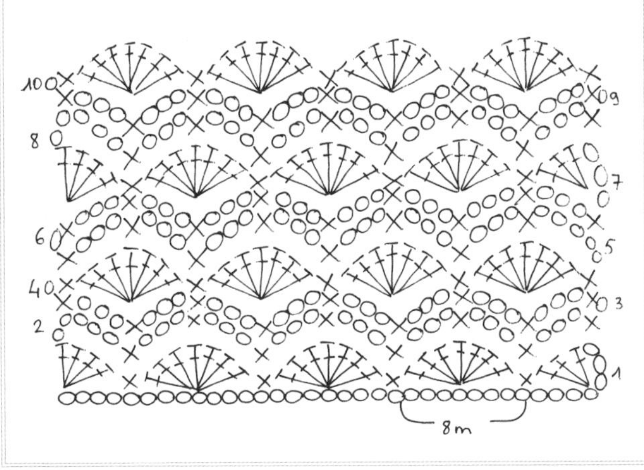

✻ **shell stitch**

CHAPTER 3

lesson 17

STARTING LACE STITCHES

LESSON 17

HAZELNUT STITCH

project: make a beret

directions → pages 154–156 • assembly → page 157 • variation → page 158

MATERIALS:

2 skeins of sportweight yarn, 100% wool, 200 yd (180m), 1¾ oz (50g), in beige (2)

Size E-4 (3.5mm) crochet hook

Scissors

Yarn needle

Straight pins

STITCHES USED

Single crochet

Double crochet

Hazelnut stitch

SIZE

One size

GAUGE

20 stitches = 4" (10cm) wide

22 rows = 4" (10cm) high

DIMENSIONS

19¼" circumference (49cm)

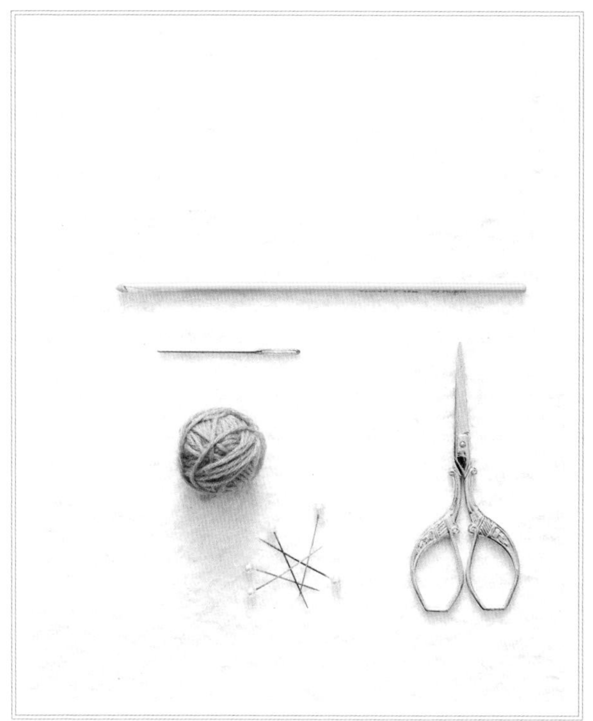

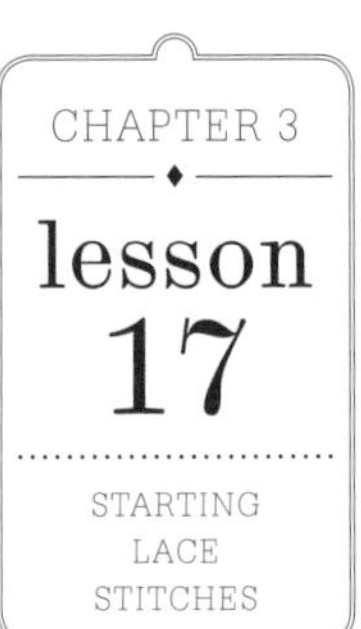

1/ starting the beret

→ **WORD OF ADVICE!**
The beret is worked flat. The crocheted band is sewn closed at the end.

1 Make a chain of 96 stitches. **For rows 1–5**, ch 1 to turn and work each row in sc.

2 Start **row 6** by chaining 3, dc 1 in the following 2 stitches.

3 *Make an increase as follows: Work 5 double crochets in the next stitch.

4 Work dc 1 in the next 9 stitches*. Repeat from * to * 9 times total. End the row by dc 1 in each of the last 3 stitches of the row.

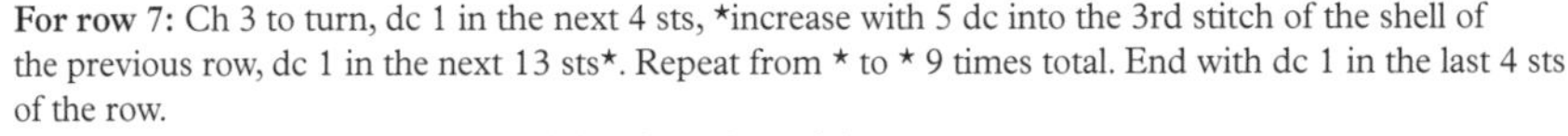

For row 7: Ch 3 to turn, dc 1 in the next 4 sts, *increase with 5 dc into the 3rd stitch of the shell of the previous row, dc 1 in the next 13 sts*. Repeat from * to * 9 times total. End with dc 1 in the last 4 sts of the row.
For rows 8 and 9: Ch 3 to turn, and dc 1 in each st of the row.
For row 10: Ch 3 to turn, dc 1 in the next 5 sts. *increase with dc 3 in the next st, dc 1 in the next 17 sts*. Repeat from * to * 9 times total. End with dc 1 in each of the last 7 sts of row.
For row 11 and 12: Ch 3 to turn, and dc 1 in each st of the row.
For row 13: Start the hazelnut stitch: ch 1 to turn, sc 1 in the next 6 sts, *ch 1, skip 1 st, sc 1 in the next 19 sts*. Repeat from * to * 9 times total. End with sc 1 in each of the last 8 sts.
For row 14: Ch 1 to turn, sc 1 in next 7 sts, *ch 1, skip the arc made from the ch st from the previous row, sc 1in the next 19 sts*. End with sc 1 in the last 8 sts of the row.

5 Start **row 15** (wrong side) with ch 1 to turn, then sc 1 in the first 2 sts.

6 Ch 3 to start a hazelnut.

7 Yarn over, insert hook into the previous sc.

8 Yarn over, pull yarn through the sc, yarn over, and pull yarn through the first 2 loops on hook.

9 There are 2 sts on hook.

10 Yarn over.

11 Insert a 2nd time into the same st, yarn over, and pull the yarn through the first 2 loops on the hook. There are 3 loops on the hook.

12 Yarn over, insert a 3rd time into the same st, yarn over, and pull the yarn through the first 2 loops on the hook. There are 4 loops on the hook.

13 Yarn over, insert a 4th time into the same st, yarn over, and pull the yarn through the first 2 loops on the hook. There are 5 loops on the hook.

14 Yarn over, insert a 5th time into the same st, yarn over, pull the yarn through the first 2 loops on the hook. There are 6 loops on the hook.

15 Yarn over and pull the yarn through the 6 loops on the hook.

16 There is 1 loop on the hook. Skip 3 sts from the previous row.

17 Sc 1 in the next 2 sts then ch 1.

18 Continue by working *1 hazelnut, sc 1 in the next 3 sts, 1 hazelnut, skip 3 sts, sc 1 in the next 2 sts, ch 1, skip 1 st*. Repeat from * to * 14 times total. End the row with sc 1 in the last 3 sts after the last hazelnut. There are 29 hazelnuts in the row.

19 **For rows 16 and 17,** work as for row 14.

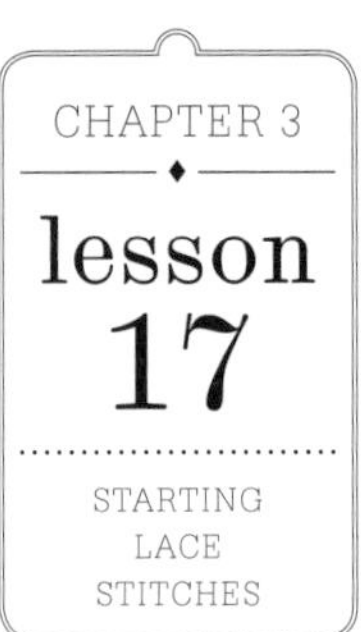

2/ shape the beret with decreases

→ WORD OF ADVICE!
On the even rows you will evenly space the decreases across. You will work 17 sc on row 18, then 15 sc on row 22, 13 sc on row 26, and so on until there are only 3 sc on row 42. These decreases give the beret its shape.

For row 18: Ch 1 to turn, sc 1 in the next 7 sts, ch 1, skip 2 sts, ⋆sc 1 in the next 17 sts, ch 1, skip the next [sc 1, ch 1, sc 1] (= 3 sts)⋆. Repeat from ⋆ to ⋆ 9 times. End with ch 1, skip the next ch st, and sc 1 in the last st of the row.
For row 19: Ch 1 to turn, sc 1 in the next 2 sts, 1 hazelnut, skip 3 sts, sc 1 in the next 2 sts, ch 1, skip the next ch st, sc 1, (⋆1 hazelnut, sc 1 in the next 3 sts⋆, repeat from ⋆ to ⋆ once then work 1 hazelnut, skip 3 sts, sc 1 in the next st). Repeat from (to) 8 more times. End with 1 hazelnut, skip 3 sts, sc 1 in the last 3 sts.
For rows 20 and 21: Work as for row 18.
For row 22: Ch 1 to turn, sc 1 in the next 7 sts, ch 1, skip 2 sts, ⋆sc 1 in the next 15 sts, ch 1, skip the next [sc 1, ch 1, sc 1] (= 3sts)⋆. Repeat from ⋆ to ⋆ 9 more times. End with ch 1, skip the next ch st, sc 1 in the last st of the row.
For row 23: Ch 1 to turn, sc 1 in the next 2 sts, 1 hazelnut, sc 1 in the next 2 sts, ch 1, skip the next ch st (⋆sc 1 in the next 3 sts, 1 hazelnut, skip 3 sts⋆, repeat from ⋆ to ⋆ once then sc 1 in the next 3 sts, ch 1, skip the ch st from the previous row). Repeat actions in parentheses 8 more times. End with ch 1, skip 1 st, sc 1 in the next 2 sts, ch 3, 1 hazelnut, skip 3 sts, sc 1 in the last 3 sts of the row.
For rows 24 and 25: Work as for row 22.
For row 26: Ch 1 to turn, sc 1 in the next 7 sts, ch 1, skip 2 sts, ⋆sc 1 in the next 13 sts, ch 1, skip the next [sc 1, ch 1, sc 1] (= 3sts)⋆. Repeat from ⋆ to ⋆ 9 more times. End with ch 1, skip the next ch st, sc 1 in the last st of the row.
For row 27: Ch 1 to turn, sc 1 in the next 2 sts, 1 hazelnut, sc 1 in the next 2 sts, ch 1, skip the ch st from the previous row, ⋆sc 1 in the next 2 sts, ch 3, 1 hazelnut, skip 3 sts, sc 1 in next 3 sts, 1 hazelnut, skip 3 sts, sc 1 in the next 2 sts, ch 1, skip the ch st from the previous row⋆. Repeat from ⋆ to ⋆. End with ch 1, skip 1 st, sc 1 in the next 2 sts, ch 3, 1 hazelnut, skip 3 sts, sc 1 in the last 3 sts of the row.
For rows 28 and 29: Work as for row 26.
For row 30: Ch 1 to turn, sc 1 in the next 7 sts, ch 1, skip 2 sts, ⋆sc 1 in the next 11 sts, ch 1, skip the next [sc 1, ch 1, sc 1] (= 3sts)⋆. Repeat from ⋆ to ⋆ 9 more times. End with ch 1, skip the next ch st, and sc 1 in the last st of the row.
For row 31: ch 1, sc 1 in the next 2 sts, 1 hazelnut, sc 1 in the next 2 sts, ⋆ch 1, skip the ch st from the previous row, sc 1 in the next st, 1 hazelnut, sc 1 in the next 3 sts, 1 hazelnut, skip 3 sts, sc 1 in the next st⋆. Repeat from ⋆ to ⋆ 8 more times. End with ch 1, skip the next st, sc 1 in the next 2 sts, ch 3, 1 hazelnut, skip 3 sts, sc 1 in the last 3 sts of the row.
For row 32: Work as for row 30.
For row 33: Ch 1 to turn, sc 1 in the next 7 sts, ch 1, skip 2 sts, ⋆sc 1 in the next 9 sts, ch 1, skip the next [sc 1, ch 1, sc 1] (= 3 sts)⋆. Repeat from ⋆ to ⋆ 9 more times. End with ch 1, skip the ch st from the previous row, sc 1 in the last st of the row.
For row 34: Ch 1 to turn, sc 1 in the next 7 sts, ch 1, skip 2 sts, ⋆sc 1 in the next 7 sts, ch 1, skip the next [sc 1, ch 1, sc 1] (= 3 sts)⋆ Repeat from ⋆ to ⋆ 9 more times. End with ch 1, skip the ch st from the previous row, sc 1 in the last st of the row.
For row 35: Ch 1 to turn, sc 1 in the next 2 sts, 1 hazelnut, sc 1 in the next 2 sts, ⋆ch 1, skip the ch st from the previous row, sc 1 in the next 2 sts, 1 hazelnut, skip 3 sts, sc 1 in the next 2 sts⋆. Repeat from ⋆ to ⋆ 8 more times. End with ch 1, skip the next st, sc 1 in the next 2 sts, ch 3, 1 hazelnut, skip 3 sts, sc 1 in the last 3 sts of the row.
For rows 36 and 37: Work as for row 34.
For row 38: Ch 1 to turn, sc 1 in the next 7 sts, ch 1, skip 2 sts, ⋆sc 1 in the next 5 sts, ch 1, skip the next [sc 1, ch 1, sc 1] (= 3 sts)⋆. Repeat from ⋆ to ⋆ 9 more times. End with ch 1, skip the next ch st, sc 1 in the last st of the row.
For row 39: Ch 1 to turn, ⋆sc 1 in the next st, 1 hazelnut, sc 1 in the next st, ch 1, skip the next ch st from the previous row⋆ Repeat from ⋆ to ⋆ 10 more times. End with sc 1 in the last st of the row.
For rows 40 and 41. Work as for row 38.
For row 42: Ch 1 to turn, sc 1 in the next 7 sts, ch 1, skip 2 sts, ⋆sc 1 in the next 3 sts, ch 1, skip the next [sc 1, ch 1, sc 1] (=3 sts)⋆. Repeat from ⋆ to ⋆ 9 more times. End with ch 1, skip the next ch st, sc 1 in the last st of the row.
For row 43: Ch 3 to turn, dc 1 in the next 2 sts, skip the next ch st from the previous row, ⋆dc in the next 3 sts, skip the next ch st from the previous row⋆. Repeat from ⋆ to ⋆ across ending with dc 1 in the last 3 sts of the row.
For rows 44 and 45: Ch 3 to turn and decrease as follows: dc2tog across whole row. End with dc 1 in the last st of the row.
After row 45, fasten off.

→ TIP

The hazelnut stitch, when done correctly, is regularly spaced with 3 sc between each hazelnut (look at the diagram on p. 158). For the beret, in order to obtain a rounded form, the number of stitches is modified as the work progresses. These increases and decreases to the number of stitches allow the pattern to take shape.

3/ sew the beret

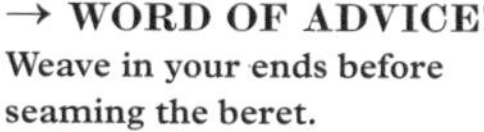

→ WORD OF ADVICE!
Weave in your ends before seaming the beret.

1 Fold beret in half, right sides facing. Pin edges together.

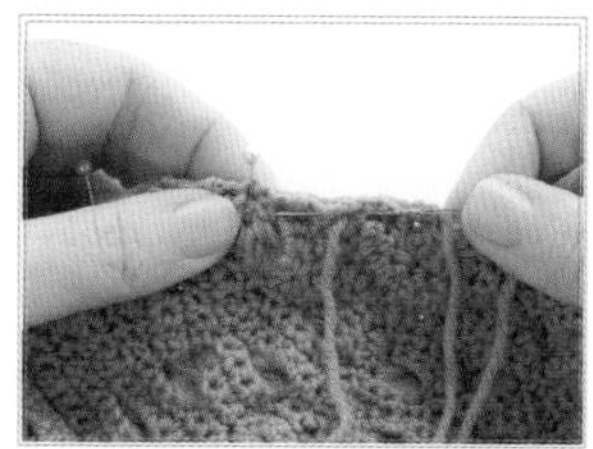

2 Sew with a back stitch (p. 68) over the back of the work.

3 Turn the work so that the right sides are facing out.

project 2: hazelnut stitch scarf

MATERIALS

8 skeins of sportweight yarn, 100% wool, 200 yd (180m), 1¾ oz (50g), in beige (2)

Size G-6 (4mm) crochet hook

Size H-8 (5mm) crochet hook

Yarn needle

SIZE

One size

DIMENSIONS

11¾" x 55" (30cm x 140cm)

DIRECTIONS

To make a scarf that coordinates with the beret, work with 2 strands held together. Make a chain of 50 sts and work with the G-6 (4mm) crochet hook. Work 5 rows in single crochet then continue with hazelnut stitch with the H-8 (5mm) crochet hook. When scarf reaches 54" (137cm) in length from foundation chain, switch to the G-6 (4mm) crochet hook and finish the scarf with 5 rows in single crochet. Break the yarn and weave in your ends.

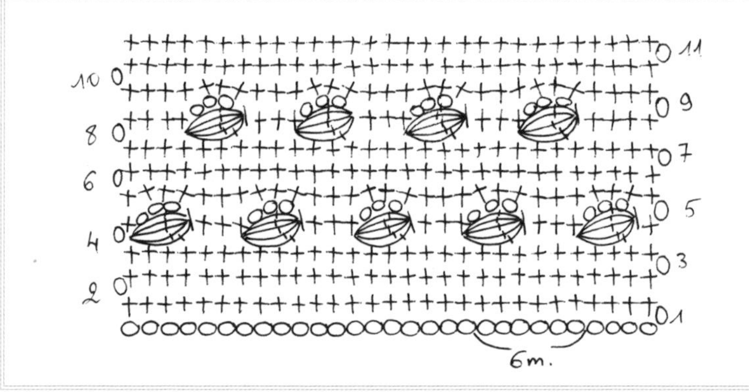

✻ **little hazelnut stitch**

CHAPTER 3

lesson 18

STARTING LACE STITCHES

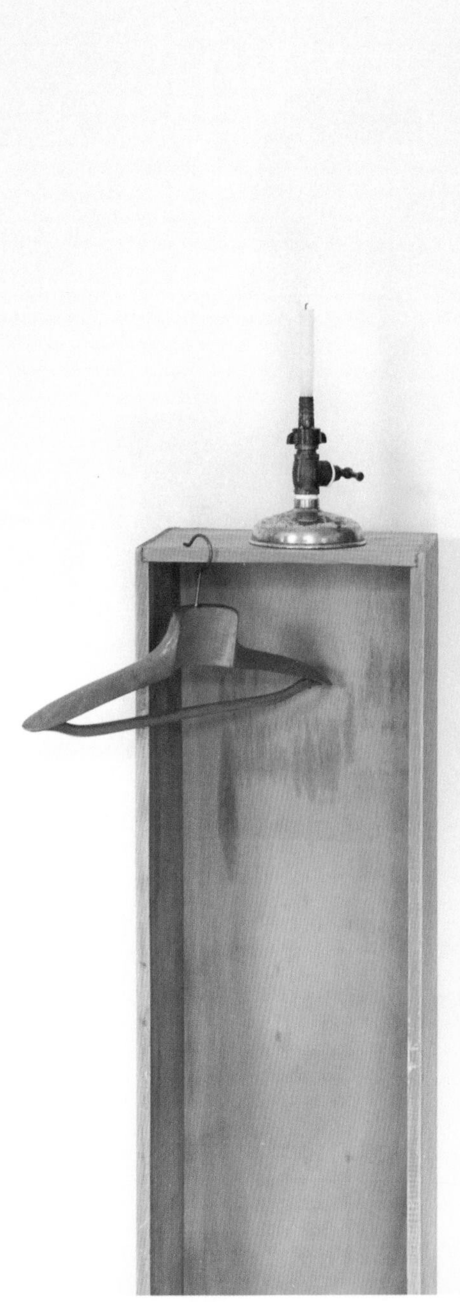

LESSON 18

PICOT STITCH

project: make a lace trim

directions → pages 162–163 • assembly → page 163

MATERIALS

1 skein of fingering weight yarn, 51% wool, 49% kid mohair, 280 yd (255m), 1¾ oz (50g), in plum (1)

Size D-3 (3.25mm) crochet hook

Sewing needle

Sewing thread to match yarn

Straight pins

STITCHES USED

Single crochet

Picot stitch

SIZE

One size

GAUGE

16 sts = 4" (10cm) wide

DIMENSIONS

27½" (70cm)

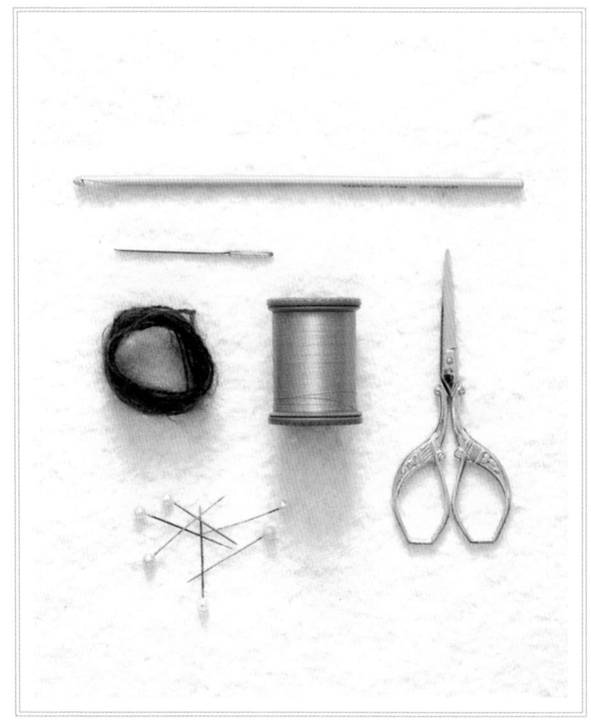

1/ make the lace trim

→ **WORD OF ADVICE!**
The picots are decorative borders of loops made, generally, with 3 to 5 ch sts each. Here, the big, decorative picots are made with 15 and 10 ch sts.

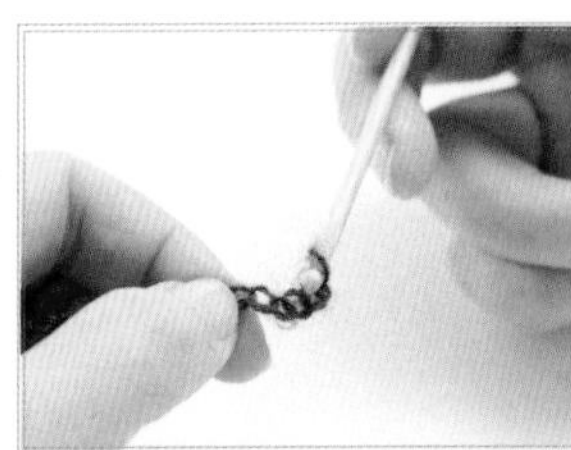

1 Make a chain of 110 sts. Turn yarn over, and insert the hook into the 2nd st from the hook.

2 Sc 1 in the 2nd st and sc 1 in the next 2 ch sts.

3 Ch 15.

4 Insert the hook into the 10th ch st from the hook to make 1 picot.

5 Make a slip stitch.

6 Ch 10.

7 Sl st 1 in the same stitch as the base of the previous picot.

8 Ch 5.

9 Sc 1 in the next ch st.

10 Sc 1 in the ch st of the next base.

11 Ch 15.

12 Make a new picot with sl st 1 in the 10th ch st from the hook. Ch 5, sc 1 in the next ch st and another sc 1in the next ch st.

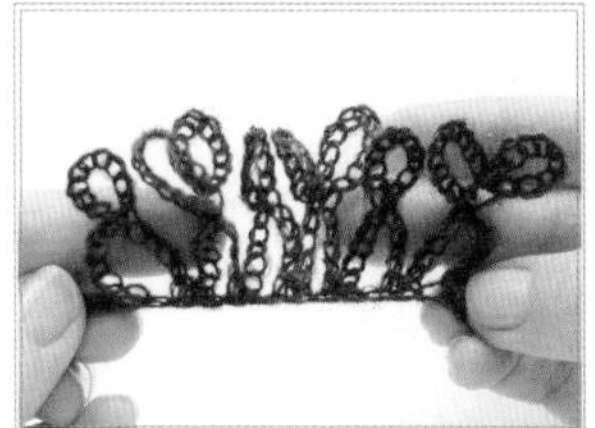

13 Repeat steps 3 to 12 across the whole chain. End the row with sc 1 in the last 2 ch sts. Break the yarn.

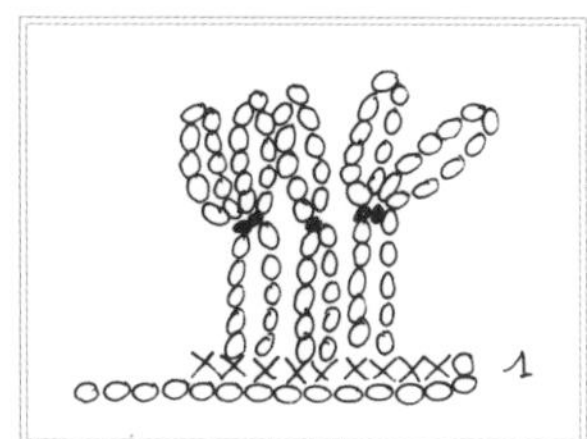

* **lace trim**

2/ sew the braid

→ **WORD OF ADVICE!**
Weave in your ends before attaching the trim to your garment in order to have a perfect border.

1 Pin the lace trim to the desired side of your garment.

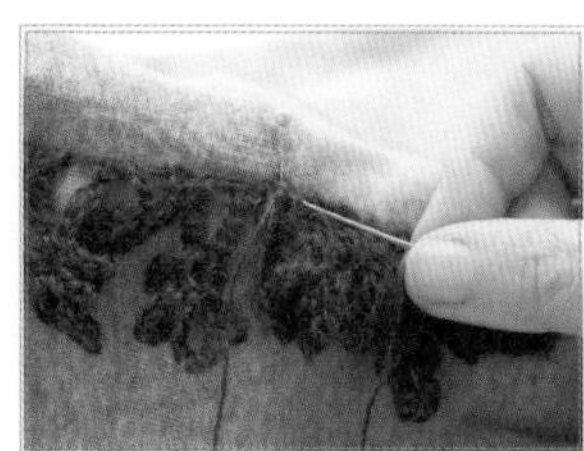

2 Secure the braid with short stitches at the base of the chain.

CHAPTER 3

lesson 19

STARTING LACE STITCHES

LESSON 19

FINISHING A TRIANGLE

project: make a shawl

directions → pages 166–167 • schematic → page 168 and 169

MATERIALS

5 skeins of sportweight yarn, 100% merino wool, 280 yd (255m), 1¾ oz (50g) in dusty blue (2)

Size D-3 (3.25mm) crochet hook

Yarn needle

Scissors

STITCHES USED

Double crochet

Half-double crochet

Fan stitch

SIZE

One size

GAUGE

22 stitches = 4" (10cm) wide

5.5 rows of fans = 4" (10cm) high

DIMENSIONS

59" x 19½" (150cm x 50cm)

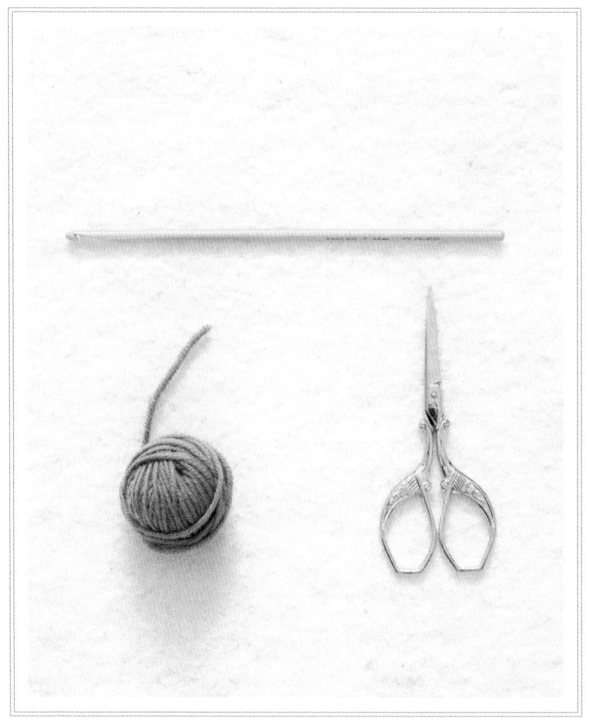

1/ make the shawl

→ WORD OF ADVICE!
The shawl starts with the longer edge. The triangular shape is obtained by decreases done with a half-motif of the fan at each end of the row.

1 Make a chain of 289 sts, or 59" (150cm). For row 1 (wrong side of the work), ch 5, then insert into the 8th ch st from the hook.

2 Sc 1, skip 3 ch sts.

3 In the next stitch, work (dc 1, ch 2, dc 1, ch 2, dc 1, ch 1, dc 1). Skip 3 sts, sc 1 in the next st, ch 5, skip 3 ch sts.

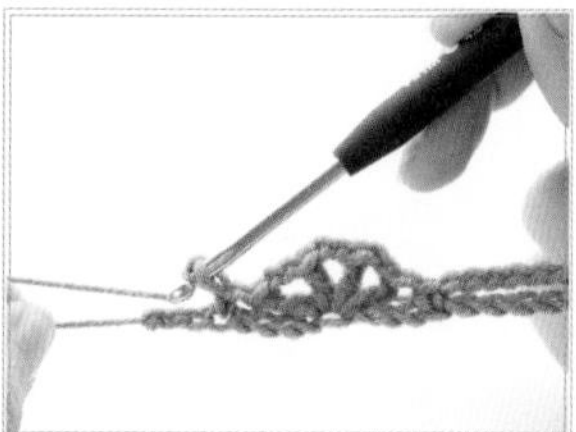

4 Repeat from 2 to 3 across the row. End after the last fan by skipping 3 sts.

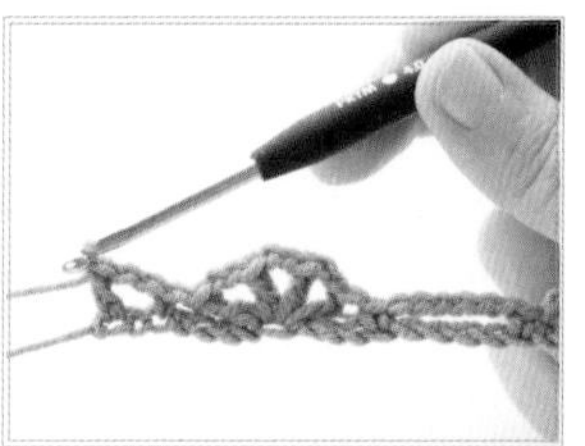

5 Sc 1 in the next stitch, ch 2, skip 1 st, dc 1 in the last ch st.

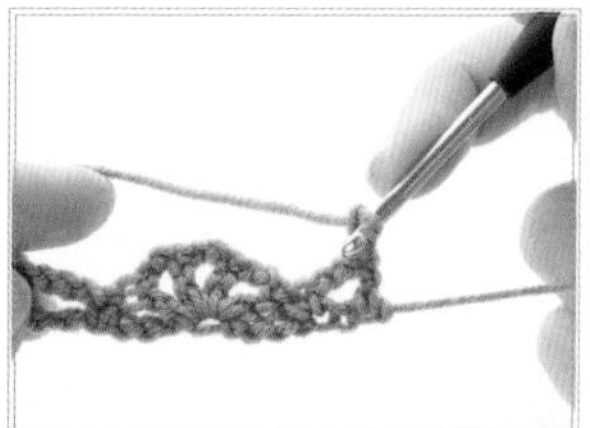

6 Start row 2 (right side of the work) with ch 3 then sc 1 in the first arc of the ch 2.

7 Continue with dc 3 in the first arc of the next fan.

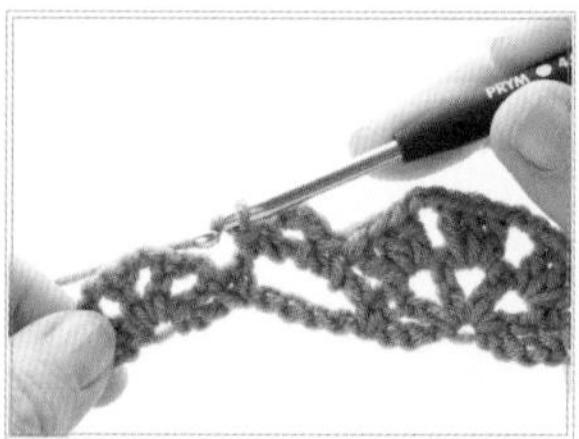

8 Next, ch 2, dc 3 in the 2nd arc of the same fan, ch 2, dc 3 in the 3rd arc of the same fan. In the arc of the next 5 ch, work (sc 1, ch 3, sc 1).

9 Repeat steps 6 and 7 across the row. End after the last fan with sc 1, ch 1, and hdc 1in the first arc of the previous row.

10 Start row 3 with ch 4, then (dc 1, ch 2, dc 1) in the first arc.

11 Continue by working sc 1 in the first arc of the ch 2 of the next fan, ch 5, sc 1 in the 2nd arc of the same fan.

12 In the arc of the next ch 3, work (dc 1, ch 2, dc 1, ch 2, dc 1, ch 2, dc 1).

13 Repeat steps 11 and 12 across the row.

End row 3 with a decrease of a half-fan similar to the previous row. Proceed as follows: above the last fan from the previous row, sc 1 in the next arc, ch 2 and hdc 1 in the 2nd dc.

For row 4: Ch 3, sc 1 in the first arc of the ch 2, then *dc 3 in the first arc of the next fan, ch 2, dc 3 in the 2nd arc of the same fan, ch 2, dc 3 in the 3rd arc of the same fan, in the arc of the ch next 5 work (sc 1, ch 3, sc 1)*. Repeat from * to * across the row. End the row with a decrease of a half-fan similar to the previous row. Proceed as follows: on the top of the last arc of the ch 5 from the previous row, sc 1, ch 1, hdc 1.

For row 5: Ch 4, dc 1 in the first arc of the ch 1 from the previous row, ch 2, dc 1 in the same arc, then *sc 1 in the first arc of the ch 2 of the next fan, ch 5, sc 1 in the 2nd arc of the same fan, in the arc of the next ch 3 work (dc 1, ch 2, dc 1, ch 2, dc 1, ch 2, dc 1)*. Repeat from * to * across the row. End the row with a decrease of a half-fan similar to the previous row. Proceed as follows: on the top of the last fan of the previous row, work sc 1 in the next arc, ch 2 and hdc in the 2nd dc.

For the following rows, repeat rows 4 and 5.

→ WORD OF ADVICE!
From row 3, work the fans repeating all of the decreases at the end of the row. To make the decreases, simply do not work the last half-fan at the end of each row.

Stop the piece once there is no longer a complete fan motif, it will be at 54 rows, or 19½" (50cm).

2/ finish by making a border

→ WORD OF ADVICE!
The decreases at each end make a staircase of ch sts on the sides of the triangle. It is on top of these ch sts that the shell border is worked.

1 Attach the yarn on the first ch st of the base by chaining 1.

2 In the first arc situated on the side of the shawl, work dc 5, *sc 1 in the next arc, dc 5 in the next arc*.

3 Repeat from * to * on the contours of the stitches of the shawl. On the point, work a shell of 5 dc. Fasten off at the end of the border. Weave in your ends.

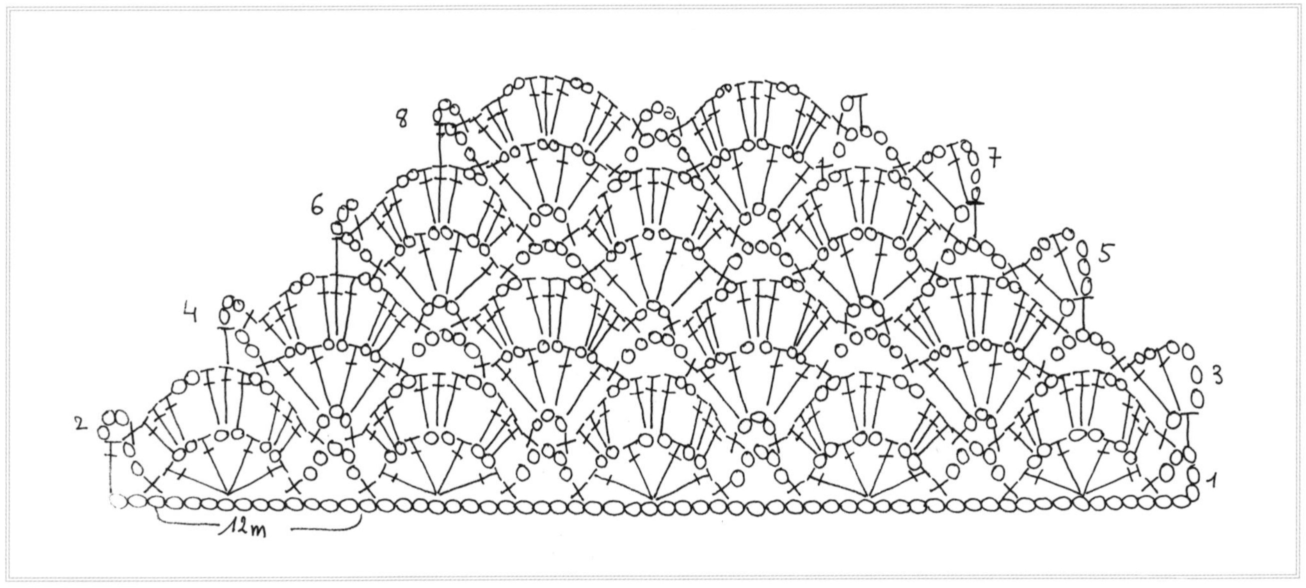

✻ **fan stitch**

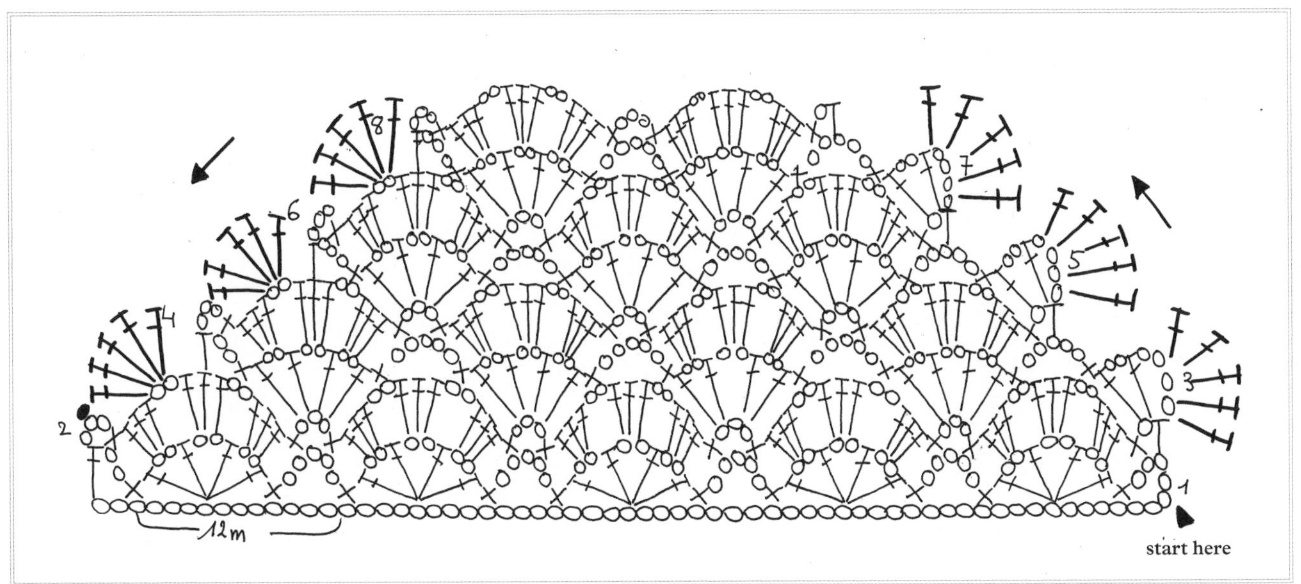

✻ schematic for the border

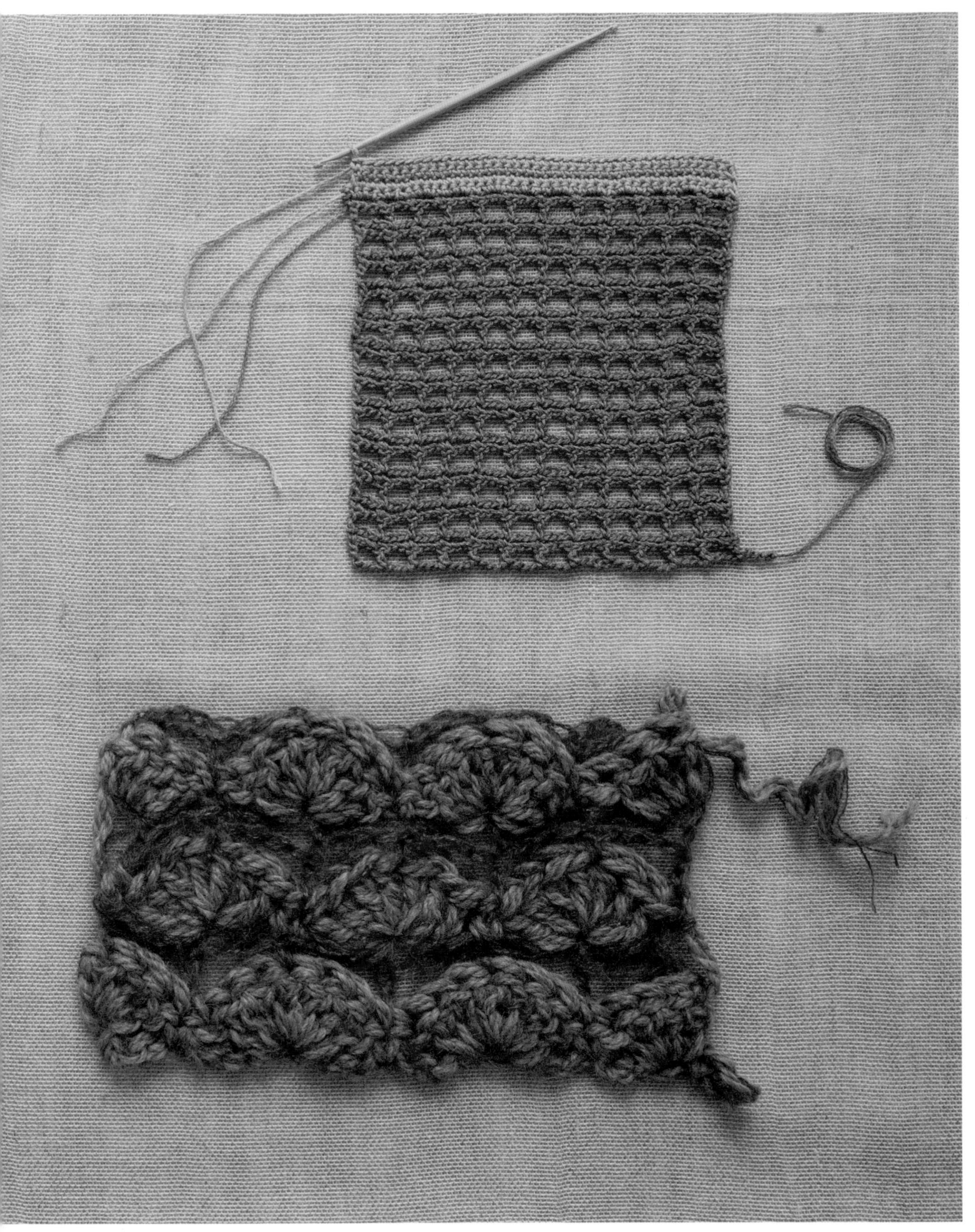

CHAPTER 4

WORKING IN THE ROUND

CHAPTER 4

lesson 20

WORKING IN THE ROUND

LESSON 20

STARTING IN THE ROUND

project: making a charm*

directions → pages 176–177 • assembly → page 177

MATERIALS

1 skein of sportweight yarn, 100% wool, 200 yd (180m), 1¾ oz (50g), in blue-gray (2)

2 skein of sportweight yarn, 55% viscose, 45% cotton, 120 yd (110m), 1¾ oz (50g), 1 skein each in brown and burgundy (2)

Size D-3 (3mm) crochet hook

12 felted beads in the yarn color palette

1 skein of brown embroidery floss

Yarn needle

Scissors

STITCHES USED

Slip stitch

Single crochet

Double crochet

SIZE

One size

GAUGE

Gauge is not important for this project

DIMENSIONS

Circle = 1¼" (3cm) in diameter

Medallion = 2½" (6.5cm) in diameter

* You will learn how to work a flat, circular motif in the round.

1/ make a ring

→ **WORD OF ADVICE!**
When working in the round, you no longer work back and forth in rows, but rather in a spiral in rounds (rnd).

1 Make a chain of 10 sts.

2 Join in the round with a sl st into the first ch st.

3 Begin rnd 1 with ch 1 (= 1 sc).

4 Work sc 3 into the ring.

5 End the round with sl st 1 in the ch st from the beginning of the round. End and break the yarn at the end of the round.

✻ **ring**

2/ make a medallion

1 Make a ring following steps 1–5 of part 1 (above). Begin rnd 2 with ch 1 (= 1 sc).

2 Sc 1 in the next 3 sts.

3 In the next st, work *(sc 1, ch 7, sc 1).

4 Sc 1 in the next 5 sts*. Repeat from * to * twice more.

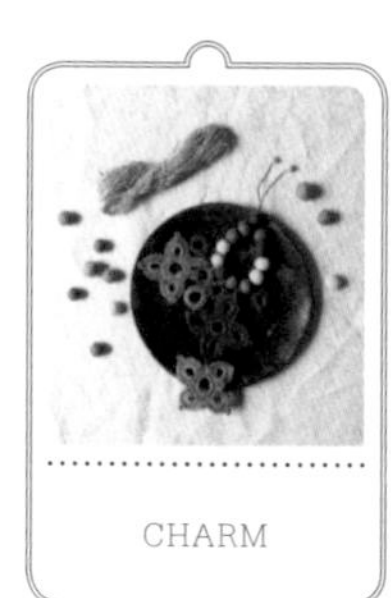

5 End with sc 5 and (sc 1, ch 7, sc 1) in the next st, sc 1 in the next 2 sts, sl st 1 in the ch st from the beginning of the round.

6 Begin rnd 3 with ch 1 (= 1 sc), ⋆insert into the arc of ch 7.

7 Dc 7.

8 Work 1 picot (loop) of 3 ch sts.

9 Close with 1 sl st in the first ch st of the picot, then dc 7 still in the same arc.

10 Skip 3 sc from rnd 2 and sc 1 in the next st⋆.

11 Repeat steps 6 to 10 from ⋆ to ⋆ 3 more times and end the round with sl st 1 in the ch st from the beginning of the round. End and break the yarn.

→ **IT'S NOT DONE YET!**
Complete 5 rings and 3 medallions to make this charm.

3/ assemble the rings and the medallions

→ **WORD OF ADVICE!**
On the wrong side of each item, weave in the end from the center only. The other end will be used to sew on the charm.

Thread the felt beads onto the embroidery floss, and join the two ends with a knot.
Thread a yarn needle with the second end from the medallions and from the circles and attach the circles with the embroidery floss between two felt balls with two back stitches.

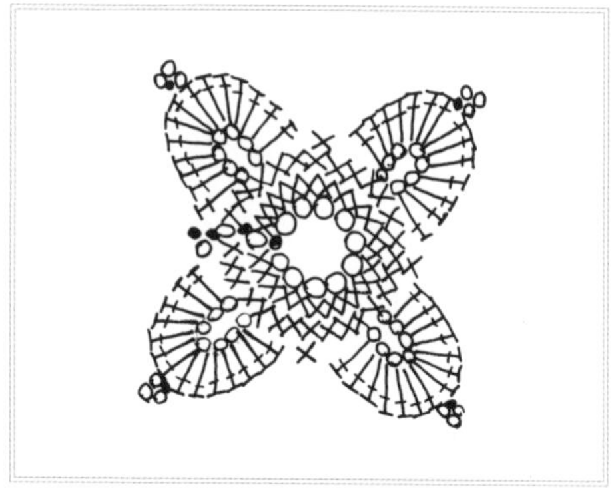

✻ **medallion**

CHAPTER 4

lesson 21

WORKING IN THE ROUND

LESSON 21

CROCHETING A FLOWER

project 1: make a brooch*

directions →pages 180–181 • assembly →page 181 • variation →page 182

MATERIALS

1 skein of fingering weight yarn, 51% kid mohair, 49% wool, 280 yd (255m) 1¾ oz (50g), 1 skein each in pink, spring green, and berry (1)

Size D-3 (3.25mm) crochet hook

1 pin back

Yarn needle

Sewing thread, in pink

Scissors

STITCHES USED

Slip stitch

Single crochet

Half-double crochet

Double crochet

SIZE

One size

GAUGE

Gauge is not important for this project

DIMENSIONS

Flower = 2¾" (7cm) in diameter

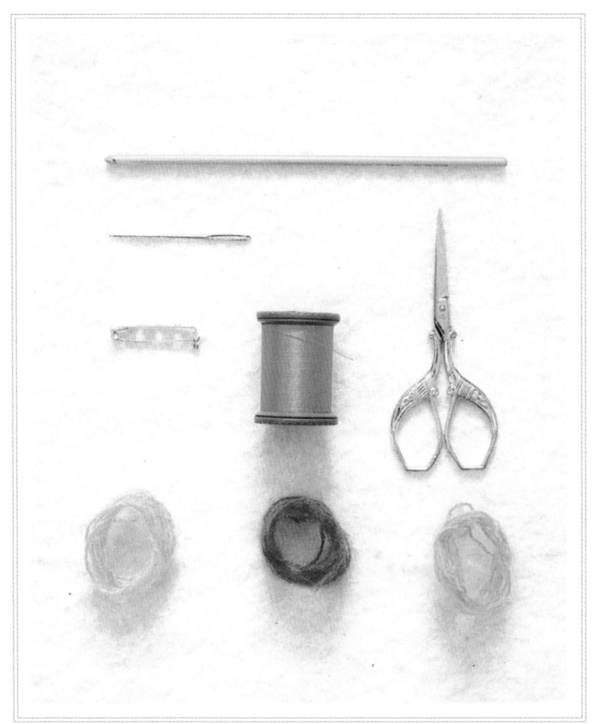

* To master this technique, you will learn how to crochet a flower with layered petals.

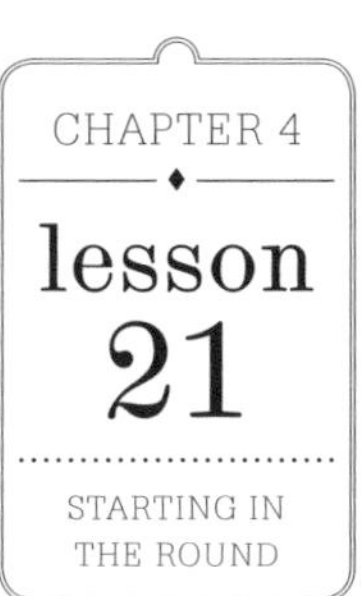

1/ make a layered flower

→ **WORD OF ADVICE!**
This motif can be worked with a single color or by changing colors. Changing yarn is done at the beginning of the round, while working the chain stitches. Change yarn the same way you do when working in rows back and forth.

1 Make a chain of 4 sts, join in the round with a sl st in the first ch st.

2 Start rnd 1 with ch 1 (= 1 sc), then sc 7 into the ring. Close the round with a sl st in the ch st from the beginning of the round.

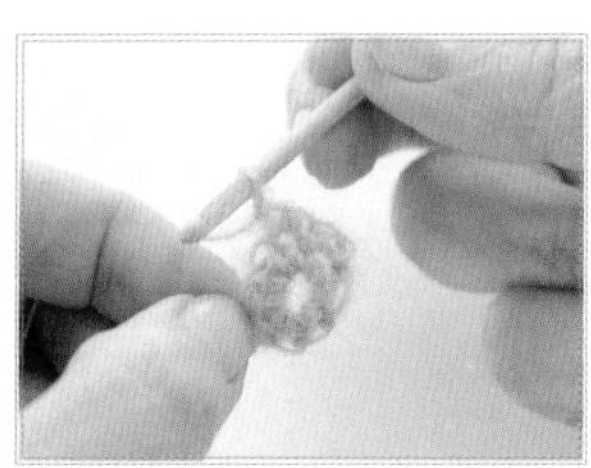

3 Start round 2 with ch 1 (= 1 sc), then sc 1 in the foot of the ch st and sc 2 in each st of round 1.

4 Close the round with a sl st in the ch st from the beginning of the round. There are 16 sc.

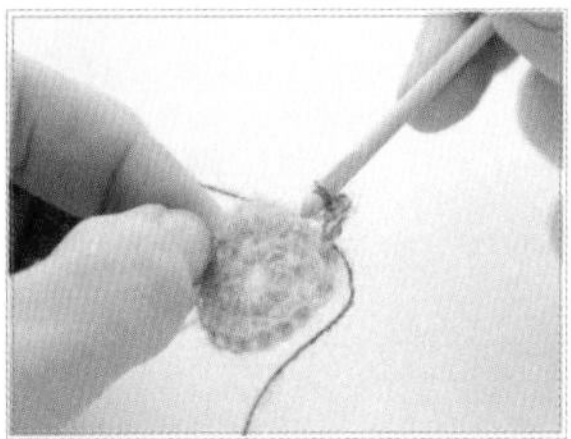

5 Change colors for round 3, ch 1 (= 1 sc) and ch 4.

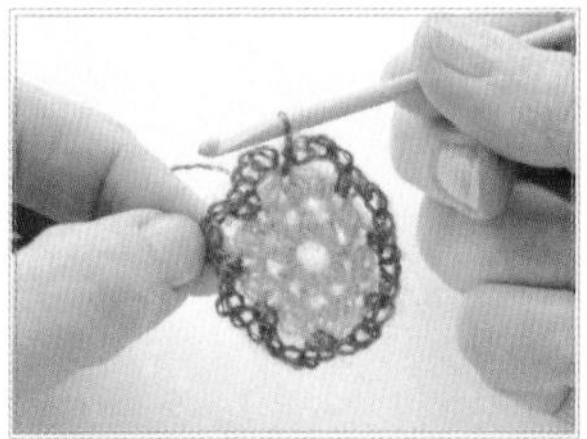

6 Skip the first sc, *sc 1 in the next stitch, skip 1 st, ch 3*, repeat from * to * across the round and end with ch 3 and sl st in the first ch st from the beginning of the round.

7 Start round 4 by working ch 1 (= 1 sc), *in the next arc work (sc 1, hdc 1, dc 1, hdc 1, sc 1)*.

8 Repeat from * to * in each arc of the round (8 times total). End the round with a sl st in the ch st from the beginning of the round.

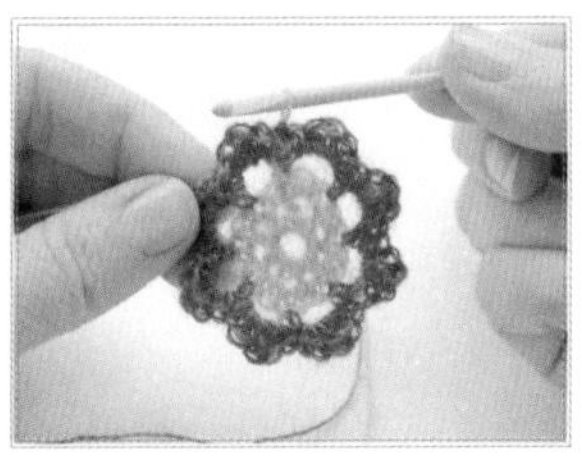

9 Change colors for round 5, ch 1.

10 Fold the petals of the previous round towards the front.

11 Dc 1 by passing the hook around the first sc from rnd 3.

BROOCH

12 ⋆Ch 3

13 Dc 1 around the sc of the next arc. Repeat from ⋆ to ⋆ across the row. End with ch 3, sl st in the ch st from the beginning of the round.

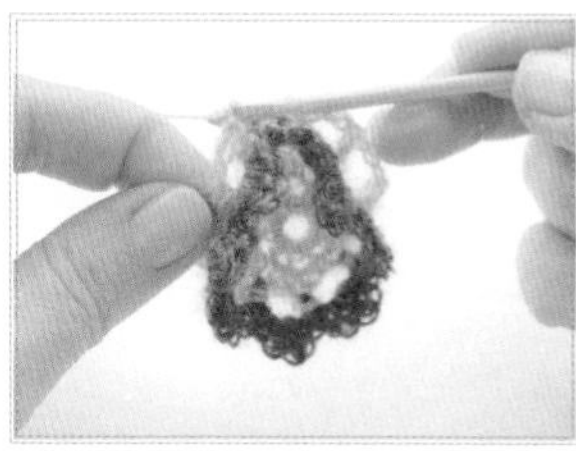

14 There are 8 arcs placed under the first row of petals.

15 For row 6, ch 1 ⋆in the next arc work (sc 1, hdc 1, dc 3, hdc 1, sc 1⋆. Repeat from ⋆ to ⋆ 8 times in total and end with a sl st in the ch st from the beginning of the round.

16 Change colors for row 7. Ch 1.

17 Fold the petals of the previous rounds towards the front and dc 1 by passing the hook around the first dc from round 5.

18 ⋆Ch 5, dc 1 around the dc of the next arc⋆. Repeat from ⋆ to ⋆ across the round. End with ch 5, sl st in the ch st from the beginning of the round. There are 8 arcs.

19 Start rnd 8 with ch 1, then ⋆in the next arc work (sc 1, hdc 1, dc 5, hdc 1, sc 1)⋆. Repeat from ⋆ to ⋆ 8 times total and end with a sl st in the ch st from the beginning of the round. End and break the yarn at the end of rnd 8.

2/ finish

→ WORD OF ADVICE!
Carefully weave in your ends.

For the brooch, sew a pin back to the back of a flower with sewing thread using backstitch (p. 67).

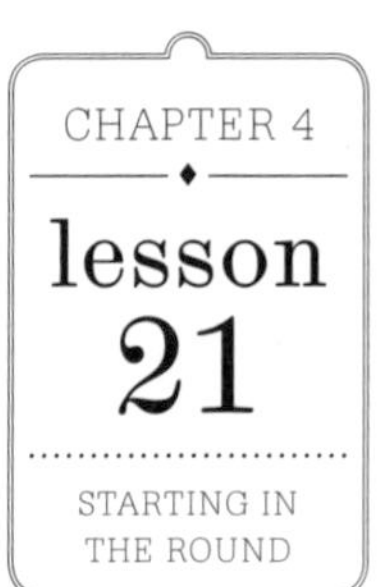

project 2: the bracelet

MATERIALS

1 skein of fingering weight yarn, 51% kid mohair, 49% wool, 280 yd (255m) 1¾ oz (50g), 1 skein each in pink, spring green, and berry (1)

Size D-6 (3mm) crochet hook

Yarn needle

Scissors

SIZE

One size

DIRECTIONS

Make 3 flowers switching up the colors.
Flower 1 = berry + pink + spring green + berry
Flower 2 = pink + spring green + berry + pink
Flower 3 = spring green + berry + pink + spring green

To make the bracelet, thread a needle and with small back stitches sew two outer petals of one flower to two outer petals of another flower. Assemble three flowers total, closing to make a circle.

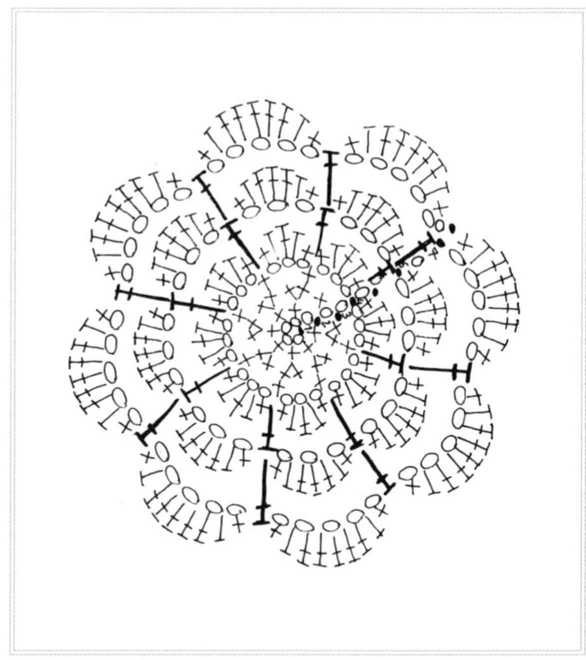

✻ **flower**

CHAPTER 4

lesson 22

WORKING IN THE ROUND

LESSON 22

ASSEMBLING MOTIFS

project 1: make a capelet*

directions → pages 186–187 • assembly → page 188 • schematics → pages 188 and 189 • variations → pages 190, 192, and 194

MATERIALS

3 skeins of fingering weight yarn, 51% wool, 49% kid mohair, 280 yd (255m), 1¾ oz (50g), in pale gray (1)

Size D-3 (3mm) crochet hook

Yarn needle

Scissors

Straight pins

STITCHES USED

Slip stitch

Single crochet

5-stitch puff

SIZE

One size

GAUGE

Flower = 2¼" (5.5cm) in diameter

DIMENSIONS

19¾" wide x 11" high (50cm x 28cm)

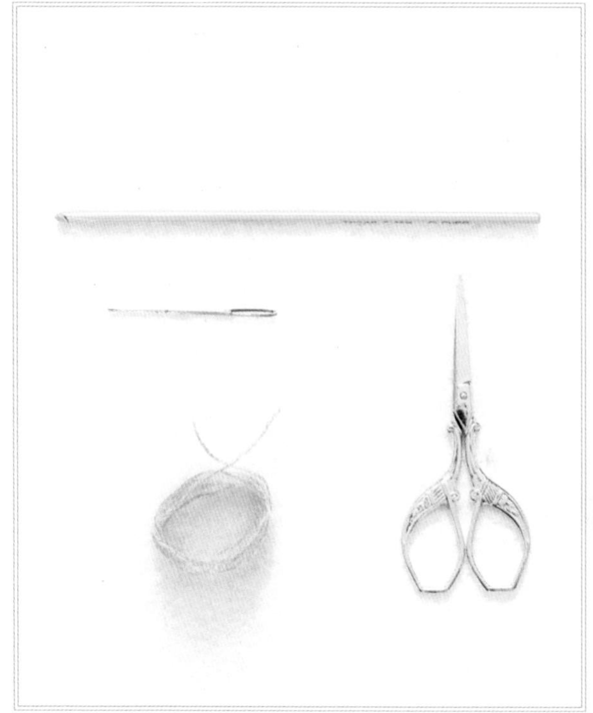

* Learn to assemble the anemone motifs in order to make scarves, headbands, and other accessories.

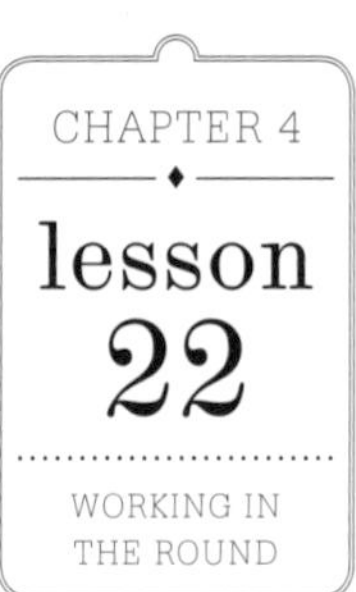

1/ make an anemone flower

→ **WORD OF ADVICE!**
The puffs give the petal of the anemone its shape.

1 Make a chain of 6 stitches. Join in the round with a sl st in the first ch st.

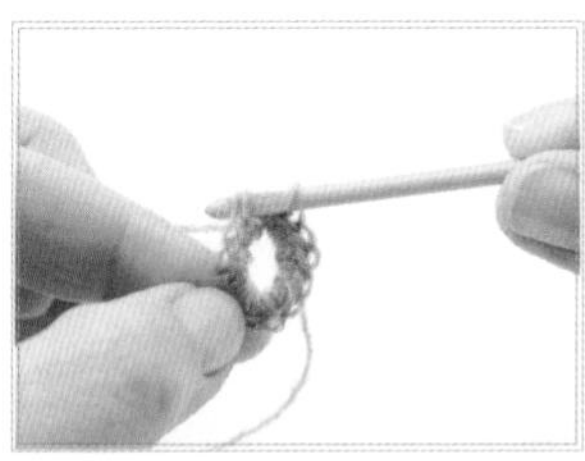

2 Start rnd 1 with ch 1 (= 1 sc) and sc 12 into the circle.

3 End the round with 1 sl st in the ch st from the beginning of the round.

4 Start rnd 2 with ch 1, then sc 1 in the first sc of the previous round. *Ch 3, skip 1 st, sc 1 in the next st*.

5 Repeat from * to * across the round. End with ch 3 and sl st in the ch st from the beginning of the round. There are 6 arcs.

6 Start round 3 with ch 5.

7 In the next arc, in order to make a puff, yarn over, and insert the hook into the arc.

8 Yarn over.

9 Pull the loop through the arc, stretching it out some. There are 3 loops on the hook.

10 Yarn over, and insert the hook into the arc.

11 Yarn over, and pull the loop, stretching it out. There are 5 loops on the hook.

12 Repeat steps 10 and 11 five times total. There are 11 loops on the hook.

13 Yarn over.

14 Pull the yarn over through all 11 loops. Yarn over and pull it through the loop on the hook. The puff will take shape.

15 Ch 5, sl st in the next sc from the previous round.

16 Repeat steps 7–15 in order to have 6 puffs total, one in each arc.

17 End with a sl st in the sl st from the end of rnd 2. Stop and cut the yarn, leaving at least 6" (15cm) of yarn.

2/ it's not done yet!

For the capelet, you need to make 78 anemones.
Weave in the end from the center of the motif.
The other end will be used to seam the anemones together.

* one anemone

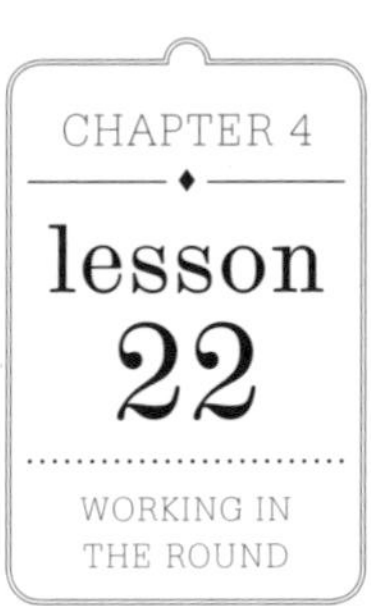

3/ assemble the capelet

Following the assembly schematic, arrange the first row of the back by aligning the nine motifs of the bottom in a row. Assemble the anemones of this entire row by sewing them side by side, the two petals of one flower against two petals of its neighbor, with 2 back stitches using the loose strands. Hide any unsightly strands by weaving the needle through the puff of the next petal toward the back of the motif.

Continue the piece with a row placed above, composed of eight motifs. Assemble the eight motifs in a row as you did for the previous row.

Repeat for the other rows until there are six rows. Then arrange the rows from shortest to longest so that the motifs interlock. Assemble the rows using back stitches to secure the petals.

Make the front as the back.

Place the back and the front together, wrong sides facing. Sew the anemone petals at the sides in the same way.

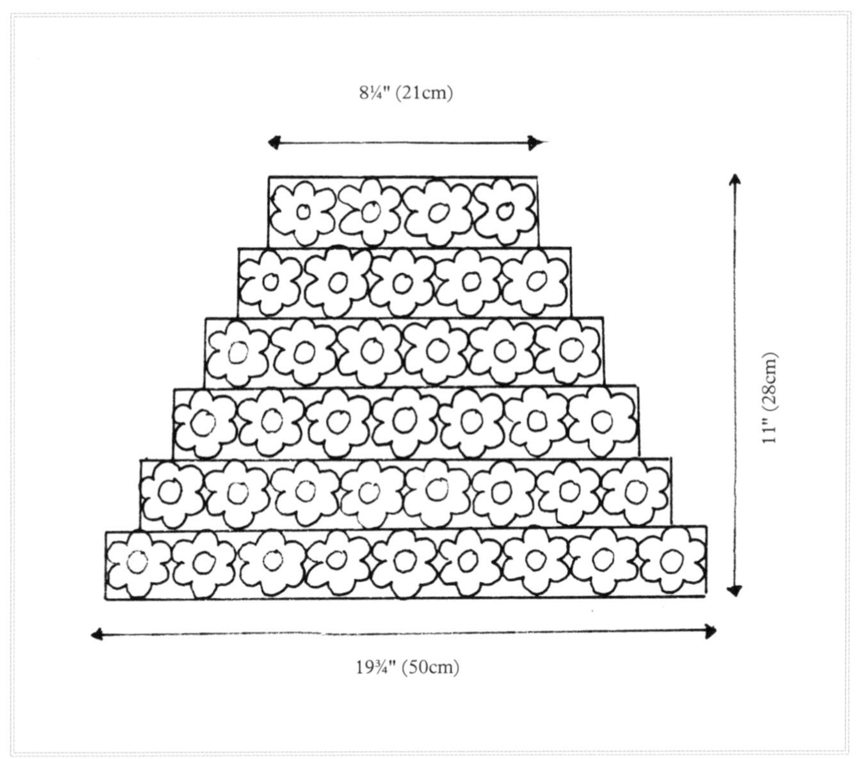

* placement schematic

✻ **assembly schematic**

project 2: the headband

MATERIALS

1 skein of fingering weight yarn, 51% combed wool, 49% kid mohair, 280 yd (255m), 1¾ oz (50g), in pale pink (1)

Size D-3 (3mm) crochet hook

Yarn needle

Scissors

SIZE

One size

DIMENSIONS

9" circumference x 7½" high (23cm x 19cm)

DIRECTIONS

Crochet 32 motifs. Arrange 4 rows of 8 anemones by staggering them (as for the capelet on page 188) and assemble them with backstitch.
The rectangle measures 18" (46cm) x 7½" (19cm).
Fold the band in half and sew the flower petals located at the two ends together.

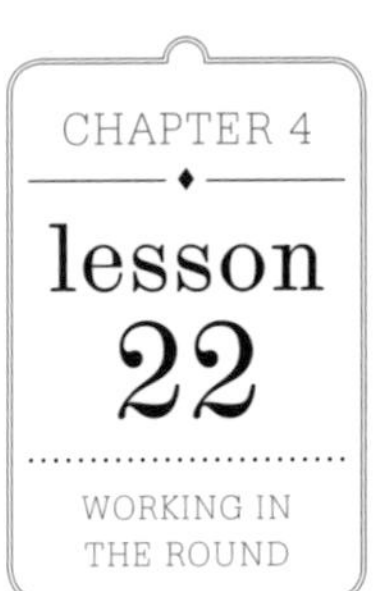

project 3: the floral wrap

MATERIALS

2 skeins of fingering weight yarn, 51% wool, 49% kid mohair, 280 yd (255m), 1¾ oz (50g), in off-white, and 1 skein each in pale gray and pale pink (1)

Size D-3 (3mm) crochet hook

Yarn needle

Scissors

SIZE

One size

DIMENSIONS

8½" x 35½" (22cm x 88cm)

DIRECTIONS

Crochet 51 anemone motifs in off-white, 19 motifs in pale gray, and 19 motifs in pale pink. Arrange 10 bands of 5 anemones by staggering them as follows: off-white + pale gray + off-white + pale pink + off-white. Make 9 rows of 5 anemones as follows: off-white + pale pink + off-white + pale gray + off-white. To finish, assemble the 19 bands together, alternating colors, in order to make the wrap.

project 4: the floral scarf

MATERIALS

2 skeins of fingering weight yarn, 51% wool, 49% kid mohair, 280 yd (255m), 1¾ oz (50g), in coral (1)

Size H-8 (5mm) crochet hook

Yarn needle

Scissors

SIZE

One size

DIMENSIONS

56" x 8" (142cm x 20.5cm)

DIRECTIONS

Crochet 28 motifs working with 2 strands held together. Assemble the motifs in pairs, then sew these pairs one on top of the other as pictured, securing with backstitch.

CHAPTER 4

lesson 23

WORKING IN THE ROUND

LESSON 23

GRANNY SQUARE

project: make a vest*

directions → pages 198–200 • assembly → page 200 • schematics → page 202 and 203

MATERIALS

12 skeins of fingering weight yarn,
100% merino wool, 280 yd (255m),
1¾ oz (50g) 3 skeins each in olive, plum,
light green, and beige for sizes Small and Medium
or 4 skeins of each color for size Large (1)

Size D-3 (3.25mm) crochet hook

Yarn needle

Scissors

Straight pins

STITCHES USED

Slip stitch

Single crochet

Double crochet

SIZES

Small, Medium, and Large

GAUGE

Granny square = 2¼" (6cm) x 2¼" (6cm)

DIMENSIONS

42½", 45", 51½" in circumference
(108cm, 114cm, 131cm)

* Learn to make granny squares and assemble them to create a vest.

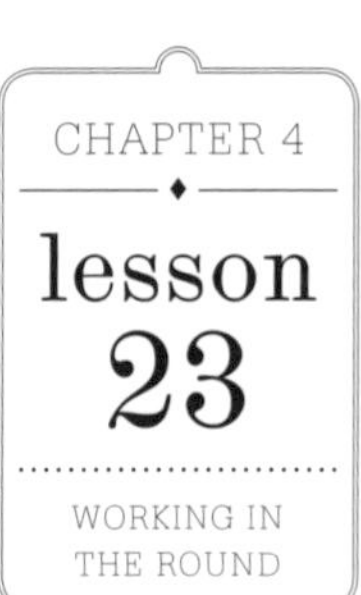

1/ make a square

→ **WORD OF ADVICE!**
To simplify the directions, follow this color code: (1) olive / (2) plum / (3) light green / (4) beige.

1 With color 1, make a chain of 4 sts, join in the round with a sl st in the first ch st. For round 1, ch 3 (= 1 dc).

2 Then, inserting hook into the ring, dc 3.

3 Next, ch 3 and dc 4 into the ring.

4 Repeat step 3 twice more and end with ch 3 and sl st in the 3rd ch st from the beginning of the round.

5 Take color 2 for rnd 2 and ch 1, sc 1 in the sl st from the previous row.

6 Ch 2, skip the 3 dc from the previous round.

7 *Sc 1 into the arc, ch 2, and sc 1.

8 Make a new ch 2 and sc 1 into the same arc. Ch 2, skip the next 4 dc*. Repeat steps 7 and 8 twice more.

9 End with sc 1 in the last arc, ch 2 and sc 1 into the same arc, ch 2, sl st into the ch st from the beginning of the round.

10 Take color 3 for round 3 and ch 1 and sc 1 into the first little arc.

11 In the next arc, *dc 3.

12 Ch 3, dc 3.

13 Sc 1 in the next arc.

14 Ch 3 and sc 1 in the next arc★.

15 Repeat steps 11 to 14 three more times.

16 End with a sl st in the ch st from the beginning of the round.

17 Take color 4 for rnd 4 and sl st 5 in the first 5 sts from the previous round.

18 Ch 1, sc 1 in the first arc, then ch 2, ★dc 4 in the next arc, ch 3 and dc 4 to make the first angle.

19 Next, ch 2, sc 1 in the next arc, ch 2★.

20 Repeat from 18 to 19 across the entire round to make 4 angles.

21 End with a sl st in the ch st from the beginning of the round. Stop and break the yarn. Weave in the ends on the back of the square.

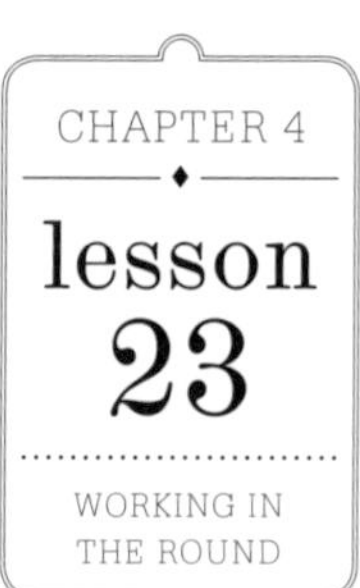

2/ make more squares

For size Small, make 169 squares, which will include 41 motifs of C, 42 motifs of B and D, and 44 motifs of A.
For size Medium, make 179 squares, which will include 44 motifs of C and D, 45 motifs of A, and 46 motifs of B.
For size Large, make 229 squares, which will include 57 motifs of A, B, and D, and 58 motifs of C.

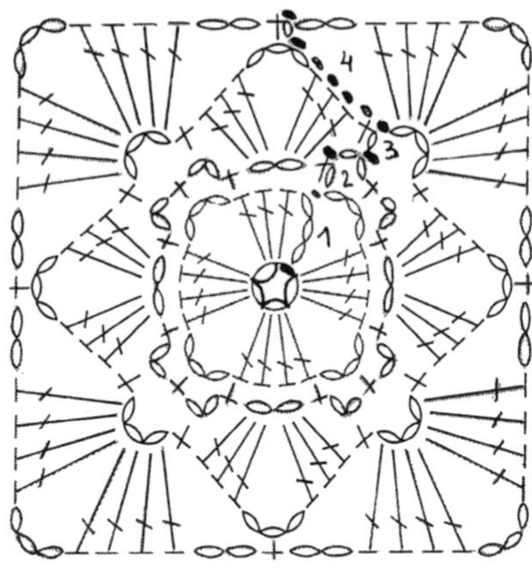

✻ **one square**

3/ assemble the squares

→ **WORD OF ADVICE!**
Closely follow the assembly schematic of the back, the fronts, and the collar in order to arrange the colors (p. 202).

Back
Assemble 9 rows of 8 squares for size Small, 9 rows of 9 squares for size Medium, or 10 rows of 10 squares for size Large.

Front
For right side of the vest, assemble 9 rows of 5 squares for sizes Small and Medium, or 10 rows of 6 squares for size Large. Make left side in the same way.

Collar
Assemble 1 row of 7 squares for size Small, 1 row of 8 squares for size Medium, or 1 row of 9 squares for size Large.

4/ sew the 4 pieces of the vest

→ **WORD OF ADVICE!**
The squares are sewn on the wrong side with backstitch using color 1.

Lay the two front sides on top of the back, right sides together. Pin the sides and the shoulder. Sew the sides with a back stitch, starting from the bottom, going up 5 rows of squares.
Assemble the shoulders by seaming 3 squares on either side of the top edge for sizes Small and Medium, leaving 2 squares (for Small) and 3 squares (for Medium) of the center for the neck.
For size Large, seam 3½ squares of each side and leave the 3 squares of the center for the neck.
Pin the collar band to the vest starting from the edge of a side, then over the back of the neck and along the edge of the second side of the vest.
Sew with backstitch over the wrong side of the work. Turn the vest so the right side is facing out.

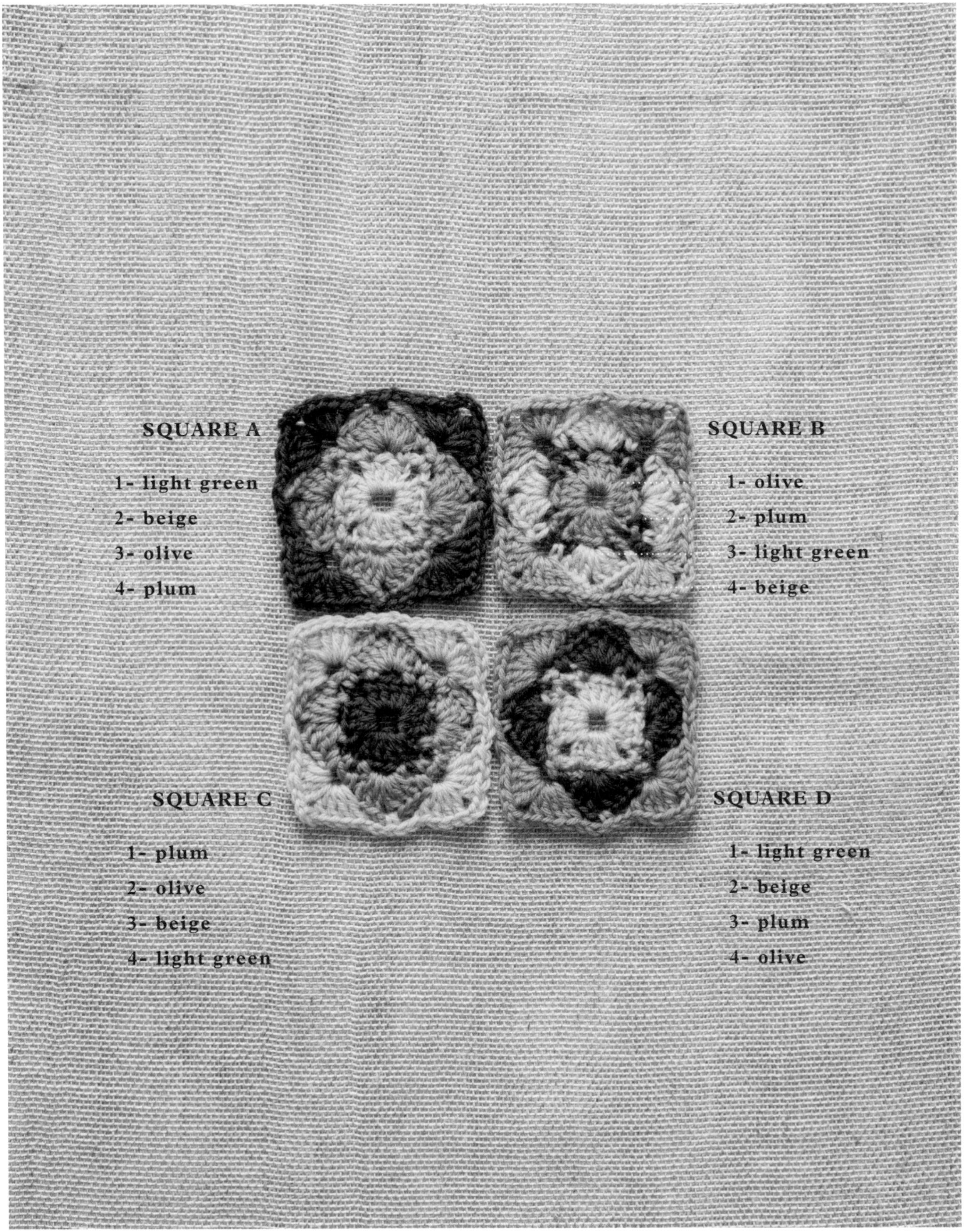

SQUARE A

1- light green
2- beige
3- olive
4- plum

SQUARE B

1- olive
2- plum
3- light green
4- beige

SQUARE C

1- plum
2- olive
3- beige
4- light green

SQUARE D

1- light green
2- beige
3- plum
4- olive

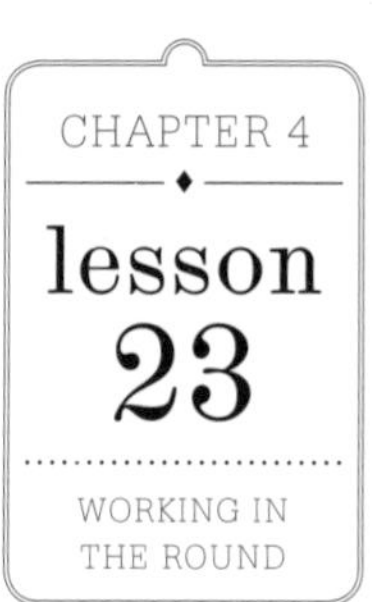

→ WORD OF ADVICE!
Closely follow the assembly schematics for arranging the different squares.

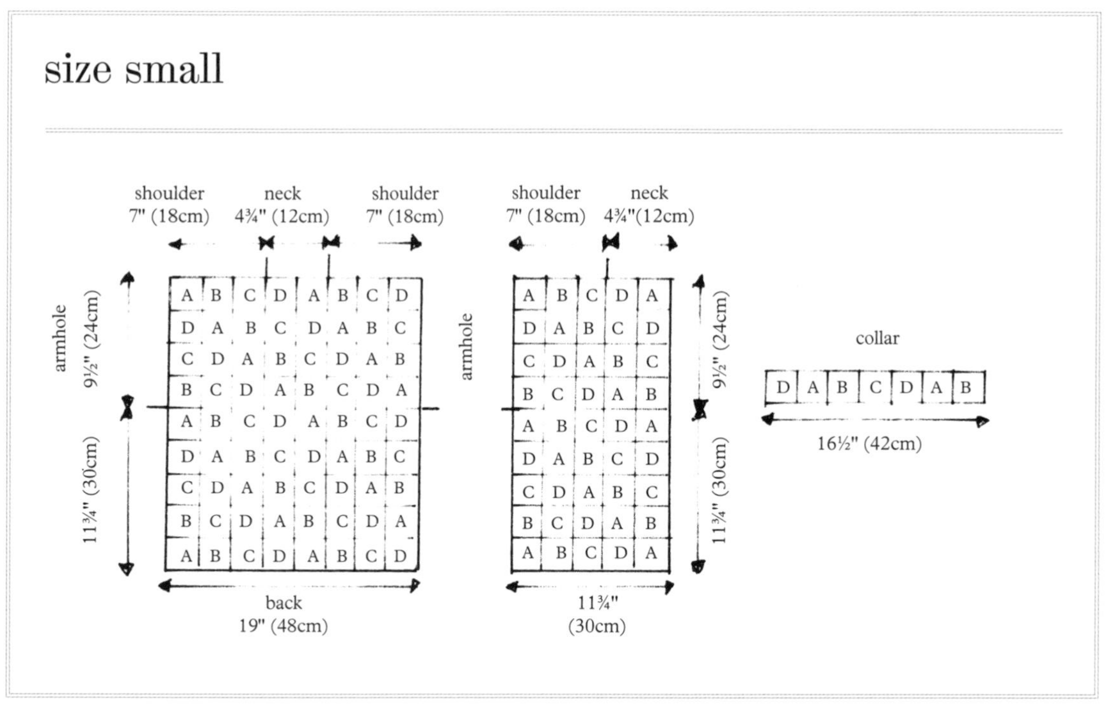

✻ **assembly schematics for sizes Small, Medium, and Large**

size medium

shoulder
7" (18cm)
neck
7" (18cm)
shoulder
7" (18cm)
armhole
9½" (24cm)
11¾" (30cm)
A B C D A B C D A
D A B C D A B C D
C D A B C D A B C
B C D A B C D A B
A B C D A B C D A
D A B C D A B C D
C D A B C D A B C
B C D A B C D A B
A B C D A B C D A
back
21½" (54cm)
shoulder
7" (18cm)
neck
4¾" (12cm)
armhole
B C D A B
A B C D A
D A B C D
C D A B C
B C D A B
A B C D A
D A B C D
C D A B C
B C D A B
11¾" (30cm)
11¾" (30cm)
11¾"
(30cm)
collar
D A B C D A B C
19" (48cm)

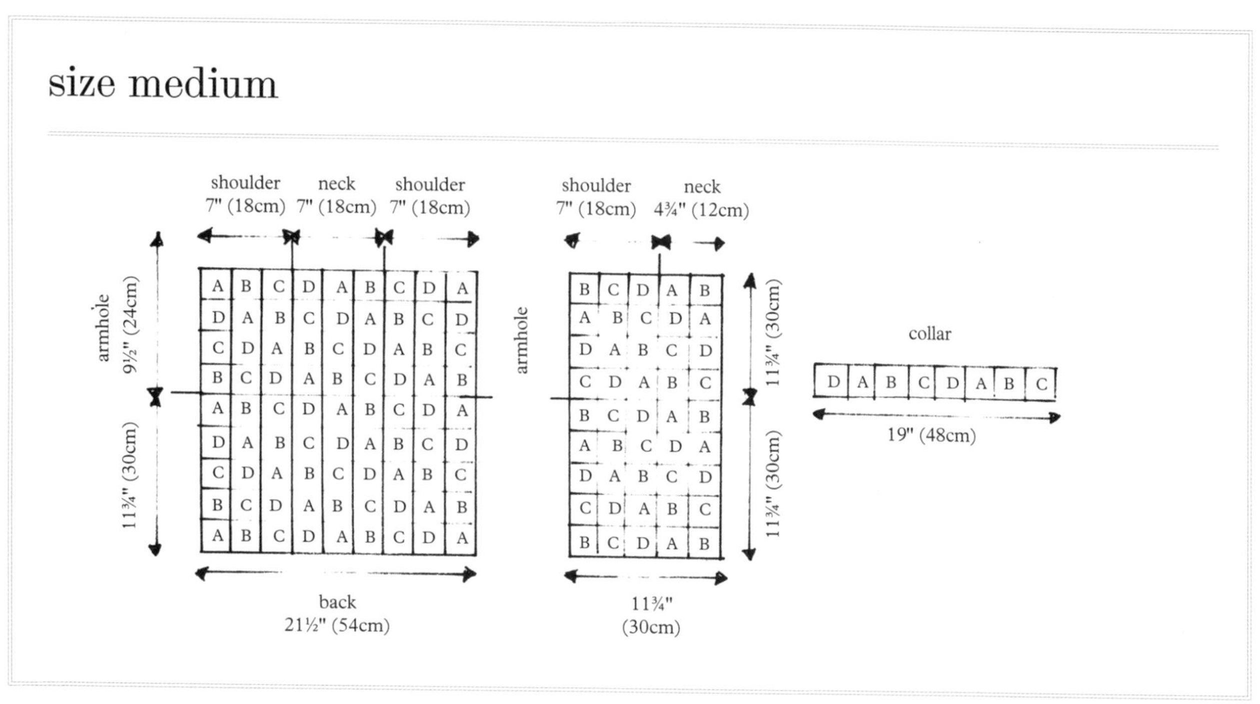

size large

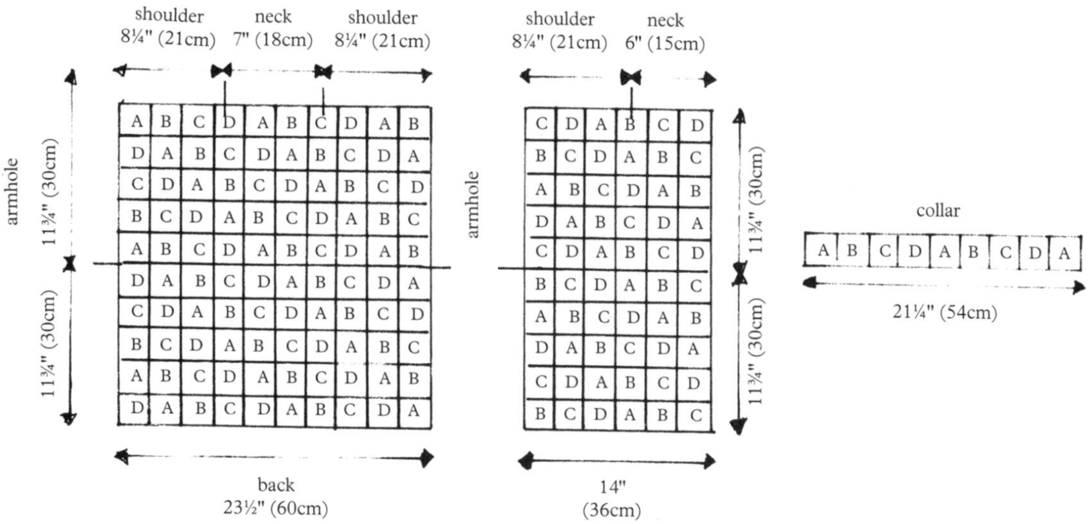

shoulder
8¼" (21cm)
neck
7" (18cm)
shoulder
8¼" (21cm)
armhole
11¾" (30cm)
11¾" (30cm)
A B C D A B C D A B
D A B C D A B C D A
C D A B C D A B C D
B C D A B C D A B C
A B C D A B C D A B
D A B C D A B C D A
C D A B C D A B C D
B C D A B C D A B C
A B C D A B C D A B
D A B C D A B C D A
back
23½" (60cm)
shoulder
8¼" (21cm)
neck
6" (15cm)
armhole
C D A B C D
B C D A B C
A B C D A B
D A B C D A
C D A B C D
B C D A B C
A B C D A B
D A B C D A
C D A B C D
B C D A B C
11¾" (30cm)
11¾" (30cm)
14"
(36cm)
collar
A B C D A B C D A
21¼" (54cm)

Modular crochet allows you to do whatever you like, whether you choose the same type of yarn to make the squares, or mix and match by arranging the colors in different ways. Granny squares are very simple and very quick to crochet, so I advise you to make some swatches before you jump into a project. It will be easier to envision the final result and you will be able to follow the assembly schematic more easily.

CHAPTER 4

lesson 24

WORKING IN THE ROUND

ATTACHING TWO DIFFERENT MOTIFS

project: make an embellished belt

directions → pages 208–209 • assembly → page 209 • schematic → page 209

MATERIALS

2 skeins of sportweight yarn, 100% cotton, 120 yd (110m), 1¾ oz (50g), in aubergine and taupe (2)

Size E-4 (3.5mm) crochet hook

Yarn needle

Scissors

Straight pins

STITCHES USED

Slip stitch

Single crochet

Half-double crochet

Double crochet

SIZE

One size

GAUGE

Flower = 3½" in diameter (9cm)

Leaf = 2¾" x ¾" (7cm x 2cm)

DIMENSIONS

51" (130cm)

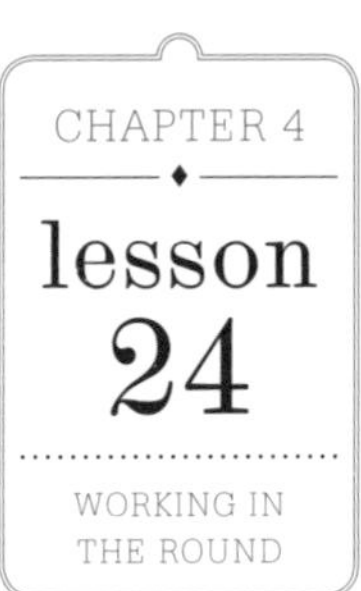

1/ make a flower

→ **WORD OF ADVICE!**
The flower is a separate piece. You need to make three flowers.

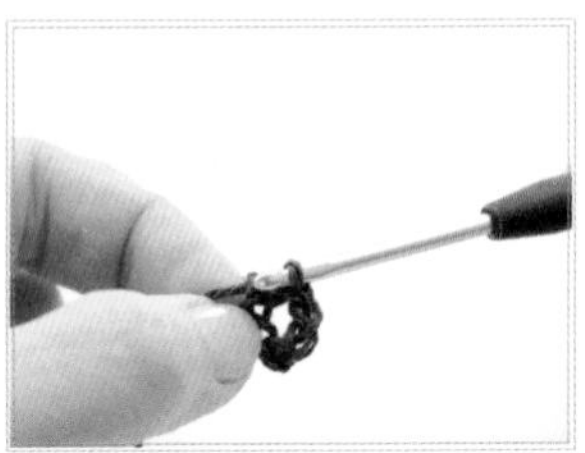

1 In aubergine, make a chain of 6 sts. Join in the round with a sl st in the first ch st.

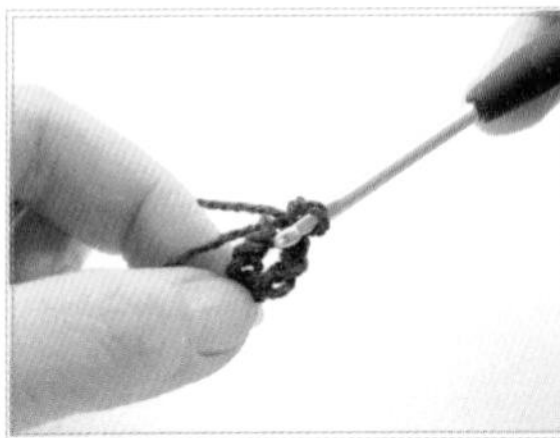

2 To start round 1, insert into the ring and ch 1 (= 1 sc).

3 Ch 12 and sc 1 into the ring.

4 Repeat step 3 ten times total.

5 End with a sl st in the first ch st from the beginning of the round. There are 10 petals. Break the yarn.

6 For round 2, switch yarn to taupe.

7 Fold the petals to the back, then ch 1.

8 Sc 1 in the first sc from the previous round and ch 6.

9 Repeat step 8 nine more times.

10 End with a sl st in the first ch st from the beginning of the round. There are 10 petals. Fasten off and weave in the ends.

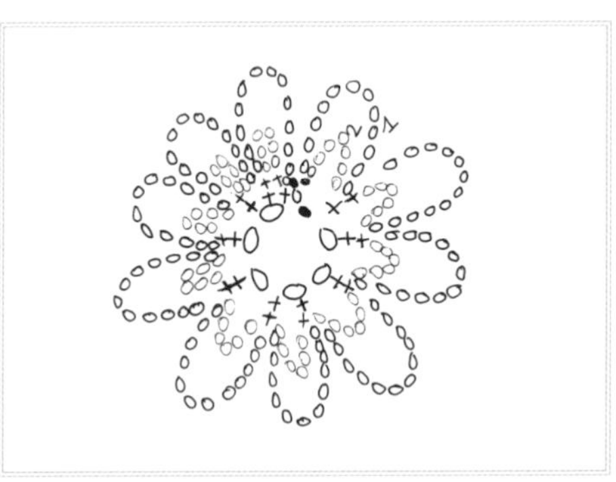

✻ **flower**

2/ make the leaves and border

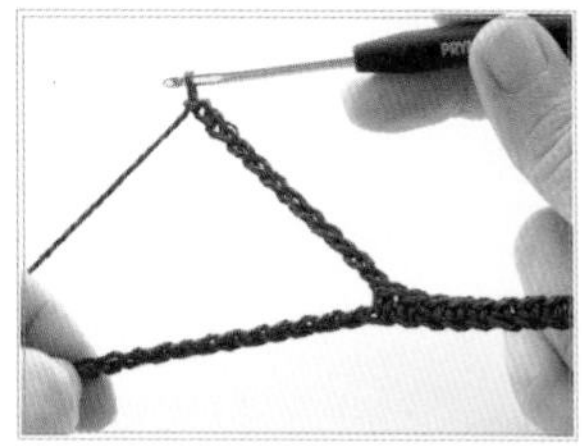

1 Make a chain of 206 sts (= 130 cm) in aubergine. Ch 1 to turn, sc 1 in the next 2 sc, then *ch 12 to make 1 leaf motif.

2 Next ch 1 to turn, sc 1 in the 2nd ch st.

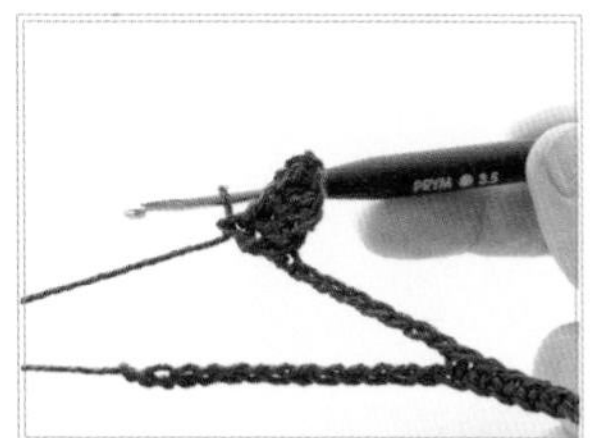

3 Hdc 1 in the next ch st, dc 1 in the next 4 ch sts, hdc 1 in the next st, sc 1 in the next 4 ch sts. You have created 1 leaf motif.

4 Picking back up from the base chain, sc 1 in the next 12 sts*. Repeat from * to * across the entire base chain, ending with sc 2. There are 17 leaf motifs.

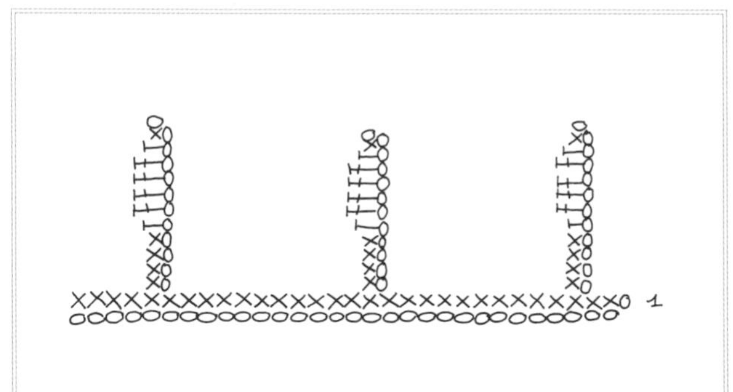

✻ **leaves**

3/ assemble the flowers and the leaves

Thread a needle with aubergine. Place 1 flower at each end of the band of leaves.
Attach the flowers to the band with some back stitches.
On one end, sew the 3rd flower in the same way between the 3rd and 4th leaves from the border.
Pin it flat on a piece of felt, and while using the cotton setting, iron it while placing a damp cloth between the piece and the iron.
To wear, wrap the belt around the waist of your pants or a skirt. Tie the two ends together loosely.

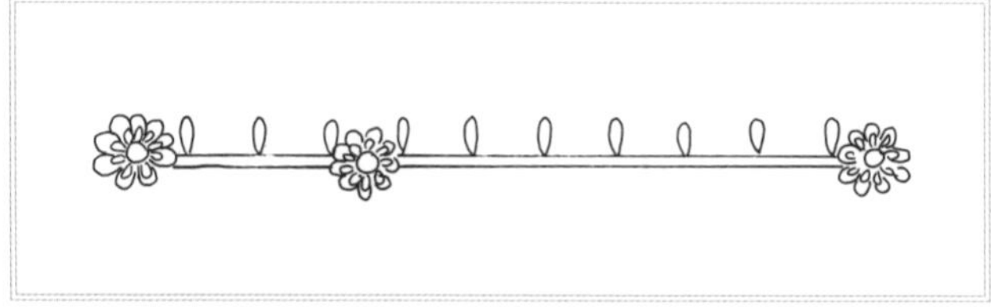

✻ **assembly schematic**

CHAPTER 4

lesson 25

WORKING IN THE ROUND

LESSON 25

WORKING IN THE ROUND

project: make a beanie*

directions → pages 212–214 • diagram → page 215

MATERIALS

2 skeins of sportweight yarn, 100% wool, 280 yd (255m), 1¾ oz (50g), in blue-gray (2)

Size G-6 (4mm) crochet hook

Scissors

STITCHES USED

Double crochet

Front post double crochet

Vertical ribbing

Double crochet worked together (dc2tog)

SIZE

One size

GAUGE

15 stitches = 4" (10cm) wide

7 rows of front post double crochets = 4" (10cm) high

DIMENSIONS

21½" in circumference (55cm)

* In this lesson you will learn how to use increases to shape a work done in the round.

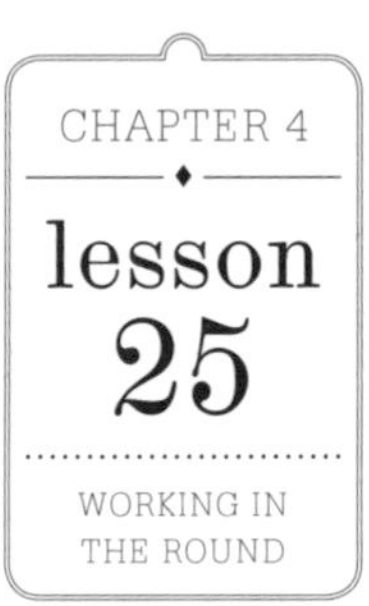

1/ the tufts

This stitch is made of tufts composed, depending on the stage of the project, of 2-st bobbles, 3-st bobbles, 4-st bobbles, or 5-st bobbles.
These tufts, from the thinnest (2-st bobble) or the thickest (5-st bobble), make up the increases in this beanie pattern.

⁎ 2 double crochets worked together (2-st bobble)

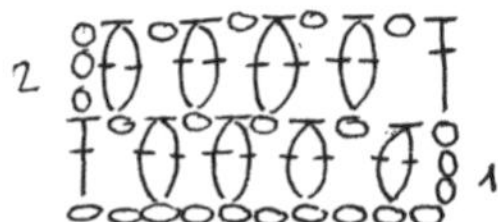

1 *Yarn over.

2 Insert the hook in the stitch, yarn over, and pull through the loop.

3 Yarn over.

4 Pull the yarn through the first 2 loops*. There are 2 loops on the hook.

5 Repeat from * to * 1 more time. There are 3 loops on the hook.

6 Yarn over and pull it through the 3 loops on the hook.

✻ 3 double crochets worked together (3-st bobble)

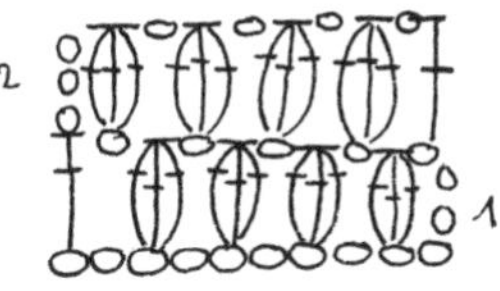

7 Repeat steps 1 to 5. Yarn over, insert the hook into the stitch, yarn over, pull through the loop, yarn over, and pull the yarn through the first 2 loops. There are 4 loops on the hook.

8 Yarn over and pull it through the 4 loops on the hook.

✻ 4 double crochets worked together (4-st bobble)

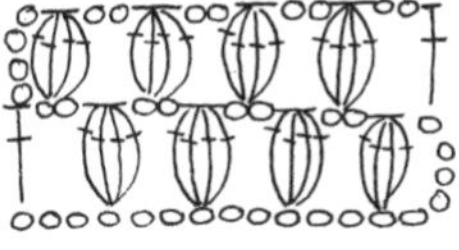

9 Repeat steps 1 to 5 and 7. Yarn over, insert the hook into the same stitch, yarn over, pull through the loop, yarn over, and pull the yarn through the first 2 loops. There are 5 loops on the hook.

10 Yarn over and pull it through the 5 loops on the hook.

✻ 5 double crochets worked together (5-st bobble)

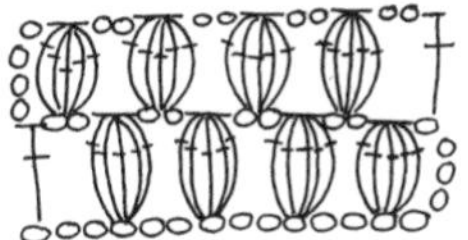

11 Repeat steps 1 to 5, 7, and 9. Yarn over, insert the hook into the stitch, yarn over and pull through the loop, yarn over, pull the yarn through the first 2 loops, there are 6 loops on the hook.

12 Yarn over, pull it through the 6 loops on the hook.

2/ the beanie

This pattern starts with the crown of the beanie and ends with ribbing. The beanie starts to take shape after the 7th round.

Holding 2 strands of yarn together, make a chain of 6 sts. Join in the round with a sl st in the first ch st.

For round 1: Ch 3 (= 1 dc), then dc 17 into the ring. End with a sl st in the 3rd ch st from the beginning of the round. There are 18 sts.
For round 2: Ch 3 (= 1 dc), *dc 2 in the next st, dc 1 in the next st*, repeat from * to * 8 more times. End with a sl st in the 3rd ch st from the beginning of the round. There are 27 dc.
For round 3: Ch 3 (= 1 dc), dc 1 in the base of the ch 3, *dc 1 in each of the next 2 sts, dc 2 in the next st*, repeat from * to * 8 more times. End with a sl st in the 3rd ch st from the beginning of the round. There are 36 dc.
For round 4: Ch 3 (= 1 dc), dc 1 into the base of the ch 3, ch 1, 2 st bobble all done in the same st from the base, then *ch 1, skip 1 st, 2 st bobble in the next st, then ch 1, skip 1 st, work (2 st bobble, ch 1, 2 st bobble) in the next st*. Repeat from * to * 7 more times. End with ch 1, 2 st bobble in the next st, ch 1 and sl st in the 3rd ch st from the beginning of the round.
For round 5: Sl st in the first ch st from round 4, ch 3 (= 1 dc), 2 st bobble in the base of the ch 3, *ch 1, 3 st bobble in the next arc*. Repeat from * to * across the round, there are 27 puffs in total. End with a sl st in the 3rd ch st from the beginning of the round.
For round 6: Sl st in the first ch st from the preceding round, ch 3 (= 1 dc), 2 st bobble into the base of the ch 3, *ch 2, 3 st bobble in the next arc*. Repeat from * to * across the round; there are 27 puffs in total. End with a sl st in the 3rd ch st from the beginning of the round.
For round 7: Sl st in the first of the ch 2 from the preceding round, ch 3 (= 1 dc), 3 st bobble into the base of the ch 3, *ch 2, 4 st bobble into the next arc*. Repeat from * to * across the round; there are 27 puffs in total. End with a sl st in the 3rd ch st from the beginning of the round.
For round 8: Work as for round 7.
For round 9: Sl st in the first of the 2 ch sts from the preceding round, ch 3 (= 1 dc), 4 st bobble into the base of the ch 3, *ch 2, 5 st bobble into the next arc*. Repeat from * to * across the round; there are 27 puffs in total. End with a sl st in the 3rd ch st from the beginning of the round.
For rounds 10–13: Work as for round 9.
For round 14: Continue the work with vertical ribbing. ch 1 (= 1 sc), sc 1 in the st of the next puff, sc 2 in the arc of the next 2 ch sts*. Repeat from * to * across the round. Close with a sl st in the ch st from the beginning of the round. There are 81 sc.
For round 15: Ch 1 to turn, sc 1 in the next st, then *front post dc 1 under the next sc, sc 1 in the next st*. Repeat from * to * across the round. End with a sl st in the ch st from the beginning of the round.
For rounds 16 and 17: Ch 1 to turn, sc 1 in the next st, then *front post dc 1 under the next front post dc, sc 1 in the next st*. Repeat from * to * across the round. End with a sl st in the ch st from the beginning of the round. Stop and break the yarn at the end of round 17.

Weave in the ends on the wrong side of the beanie.

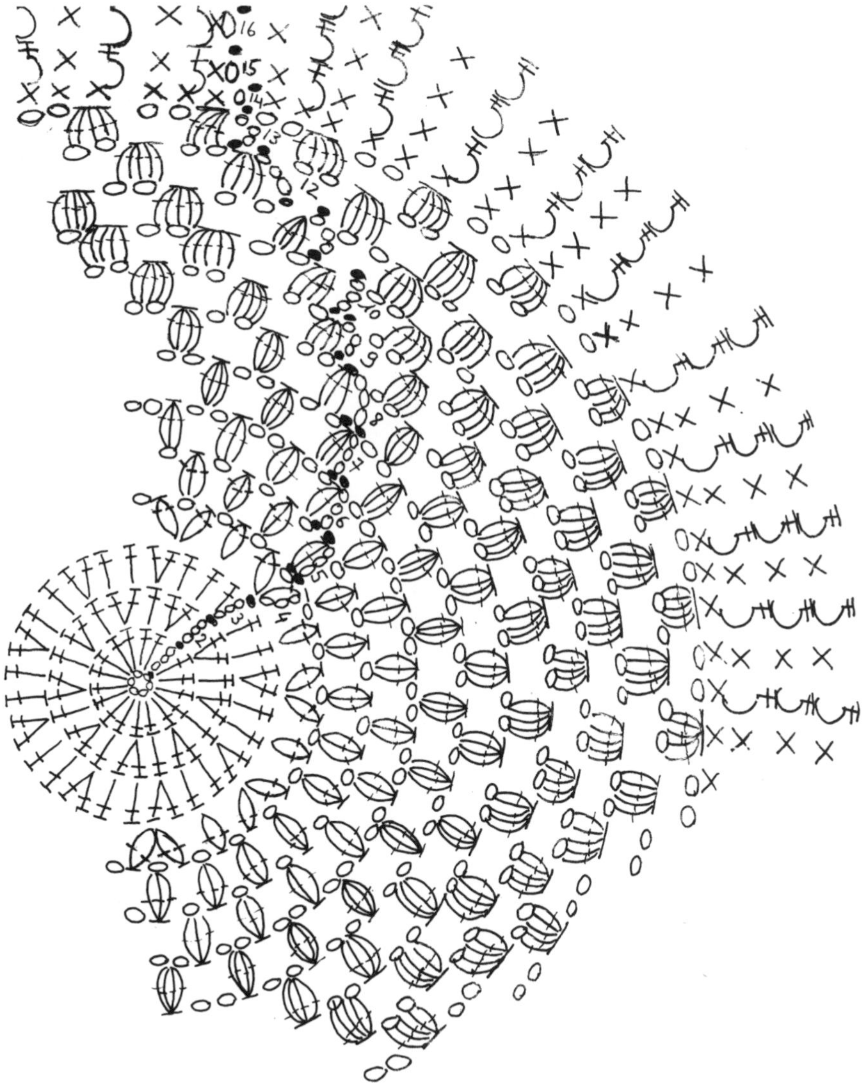

* schematic of the beanie

Index

Assembly

Symbols for clothing care

Care instructions

ironing

washing

Crochet hooks

Crochet techniques

Crochet vocabulary

Notions

Projects

Stitches

Swatches

Yarns

animal fibers

artificial fibers

synthetic fibers

vegetable fibers

Acknowledgments

My designs have been made possible thanks to the very beautiful yarns of Anny Blatt and Bouton d'Or. My very special thanks to Anne Molineau.

My wholehearted thanks to Auréa Polo for her sound advice, her expert hands, and her great smile, which accompanied me during the design and writing of my patterns. This book is a homage to her great talent.

Resources

Each pattern specifies the yarn used in the samples, including the fiber composition, yardage (meterage), and number of skeins needed. All yarns may not be available in local yarn stores, and sometimes they may have a limited choice of colors. We recommend searching several yarn stores to find the perfect yarn for your project.

You can also shop online to find yarn. These are some of the most popular online retailers:

www.etsy.com
www.handknitting.com
www.hobbylobby.com
www.jimmybeanswool.com
www.nobleknits.com
www.purlsoho.com
www.theloopyewe.com
www.yarn.com
www.yarnery.com
www.yarnmarket.com

Published in the United States by Potter Craft, an imprint of the Crown Publishing Group, a division of Random House, Inc., New York. www.pottercraft.com

Originally published in France as *Mon Cours de Crochet* by Marabout/Hachette Livre, Paris, in 2011.

Library of Congress Cataloging-in-Publication Data
Madel, Marion. [Mon cours de crochet. English]
The new crochet / by Marion Madel.
1. Crocheting—Patterns. I. Title.
TT825.M155 2013
746.43'4—dc23 2012048976

ISBN 978-0-385-34613-9
eISBN 978-0-385-34614-6

Printed in China

Translation by Ben Ross
Interior design by Nicolas Alexandre and Claire Bissara
Photographs by Hiroko Mori
Cover design by Ken Crossland

10 9 8 7 6 5 4 3 2 1
First Edition

CROCHET